The Future of the Commons

The Future of the Commons

Beyond Market Failure and
Government Regulation

ELINOR OSTROM

with contributions by
CHRISTINA CHANG
MARK PENNINGTON
VLAD TARKO

The Institute of Economic Affairs

First published in Great Britain in 2012 by
The Institute of Economic Affairs
2 Lord North Street
Westminster
London SW1P 3LB
in association with Profile Books Ltd

The mission of the Institute of Economic Affairs is to improve public understanding of the fundamental institutions of a free society, with particular reference to the role of markets in solving economic and social problems.

A CIP catalogue record for this book is available from the British Library.

ISBN 978 0 255 36653 3
eISBN 978 0 255 36681 6

Many IEA publications are translated into languages other than English or are reprinted. Permission to translate or to reprint should be sought from the Director General at the address above.

Typeset in Stone by MacGuru Ltd
info@macguru.org.uk

Printed and bound in Britain by Hobbs the Printers

CONTENTS

THE AUTHORS

Christina Chang is Lead Economic Analyst at CAFOD and is responsible for their work programme on economic and financial issues. CAFOD is the official development agency of the Catholic Church in England and Wales and works with partners in 40 countries around the world, responding to immediate needs and deeper causes of poverty. She was previously Policy Manager at the International Chamber of Commerce in Paris.

Elinor Ostrom (1933–2012) was Distinguished Professor and Arthur F. Bentley Professor of Political Science at Indiana University. In 2009 she became the first woman to be awarded the Nobel Prize in Economics. The award recognised her pioneering work on the governance of common-pool resources. In 1973 she founded the Workshop in Political Theory and Policy Analysis with her husband, Vincent Ostrom. Elinor Ostrom and her team conducted a large number of case studies around the world, examining resources such as fisheries, forests and grazing land. These studies enabled her to identify several 'design principles' for their successful management. She also developed a theoretical framework for the analysis of different institutional arrangements. Her extensive research led to the publication of numerous academic papers and books including *Governing the Commons*

(1990) and *Understanding Institutional Diversity* (2005). For the Institute of Economic Affairs she contributed a paper, 'Institutions and the Environment', to the *Economic Affairs* symposium on 'The Economic Analysis of Institutions' (September 2008). In March 2012, Professor Ostrom gave the Twenty-First Annual IEA Hayek Memorial Lecture on 'The Future of the Commons: Beyond Market Failure and Government Regulation'.

Mark Pennington is Professor of Public Policy and Political Economy in the Department of Political Economy, King's College, University of London. His most recent book is entitled *Robust Political Economy: Classical Liberalism and the Future of Public Policy* (Edward Elgar, 2011). Previous books include *Planning and the Political Market: Public Choice and the Politics of Government Failure* (Athlone/Continuum, 2000) and *Liberating the Land* (IEA, 2002).

Vlad Tarko is a PhD student at George Mason University and a Research Fellow at the Mercatus Center. He was previously a researcher at the Center for Institutional Analysis and Development in Bucharest. His main interests are new institutionalism, public choice and Austrian economics. He has published papers in *Constitutional Political Economy*, *Governance* and *Futures.*

ACKNOWLEDGEMENT

The Institute of Economic Affairs would like to thank CQS for its very generous sponsorship of the 2012 Hayek Memorial Lecture and of this publication.

FOREWORD

In March 2012 the IEA was fortunate to be able to host Elinor Ostrom for our annual Hayek Lecture and a range of other events. Throughout the day, she was engaging and sparkling intellectually. Every idea that was brought up, whether by young students or seasoned academics, brought a very thoughtful and energetic response. Quite clearly, Professor Ostrom enjoyed discussing economic ideas – even those that were only tangentially related to her research. Very sadly, Professor Ostrom died shortly after the Hayek Lecture and her husband – who worked in a similar academic area – died shortly afterwards. While this leaves a huge hole in the world of political economy, Professor Ostrom's legacy has ensured that, across the world, young academics are engaged in research examining the management of natural resources by communities.

Ostrom examined problems relating to the management of common-pool resources. These are very important environmental issues – especially for the poorest people in the world. If we have a fishery, pastureland or forest area, for example, it is important for those relying on it, as well as for consumers of products that are produced using the resource, that it is managed sustainably so that it can renew itself.

Traditionally economists have suggested two solutions to the problem of the management of common-pool resources. It has often been thought that the government should own and/or manage the resource. This is what happens with fisheries in the European Union. A benevolent government with perfect knowledge, it is argued, will be able to develop the rules to prevent overfishing and enforce those rules. But what if government is not benevolent and is subject to lobbying? And what if government is simply unable to monitor effectively? Fully specified property rights and private ownership are suggested as the alternative. But these can come with problems too, such as enormous transaction costs of monitoring and enforcement.

Elinor Ostrom showed how the community itself could often define the rules for using common-pool resources and also develop appropriate monitoring mechanisms that were consistent with the customs that characterised the way in which those communities lived. Often monitoring mechanisms would be chosen that were very effective but which might seem counter-intuitive to an outsider.

In no sense do Professor Ostrom's ideas conflict with the idea of a free economy. Although there may be some role for government, such as providing information or courts systems for the adjudication of disputes, Ostrom's observations about how resource systems could be managed were essentially observations about free economic actors at work. The community management of pastureland, fisheries and so on, and the implicit property rights that are involved, form part of what might be described as the 'free economy outside the market economy'. It has to be said – and this was clear from the variety of people attending the Hayek Lecture and those asking questions at the end – that Ostrom's ideas are attractive to those of a left-leaning persuasion. To the left, perhaps, the community management of a resource is the acceptable face of a free economy like a mutual bank or cooperative retail outlet – but it is no less free for that.

Mechanisms related to those observed by Ostrom can be seen in the context of many other economic activities. Golf clubs develop their own rules systems and methods of enforcement. Organised sports more generally have many polycentric sources of rules and enforcement to ensure that those participating can achieve certain common aims. The local village under-eleven football team is related to the very same organisations that manage the Premiership and the World Cup. For the children playing, there will be club rules, local rules, FA rules and FIFA rules all sitting alongside each other and with different enforcement mechanisms – there are, though, no government rules. Before the state took over financial regulation, the stock exchange would determine the rules by which participants in financial markets acted: this was a purely private body which would seem to have been a more successful rule-maker than the government. The UK and the USA both have a great tradition of private rule-making to facilitate groups of persons reaching a common end.

But Ostrom's main concern was common-pool resources. As she makes clear in the question and answer session published below, she was acutely aware of the serious problems facing the UK and the European Union with regard to our fisheries systems. Not just there, but in other areas too, we need to apply Ostrom's work in order to ensure that we have sustainable management of common-pool resources. Top-down government approaches have not worked. If the work of left-leaning and free market economists points in the same direction with regard to these problems then, perhaps, that is helpful in establishing an intellectual consensus.

Together with Ostrom's lecture, which summarises her brilliant work in this field, we also have important contributions by other authors in this publication. Mark Pennington, a UK academic, puts the lecture in a wider context and effectively demolishes the myth that Ostrom should be a poster child for anti-market economists. Vlad Tarko provides an intellectual biography of Elinor Ostrom and further context for her important work. Finally Christina Chang, who works for a foreign aid agency, provides an interesting example of how she has found Ostrom's ideas working in the context of a very difficult common-pool resource problem.

Overall, this excellent collection provides a very helpful introduction to the work of Elinor Ostrom which the IEA commends to those studying economics, political economy and related disciplines. It is also important for those policymakers who are trying to wrestle with natural resource problems and, hopefully, will help inject the required humility into their thinking.

Over the coming decades, Elinor Ostrom will be remembered for her brilliant contributions to political economy. She will also be remembered by IEA visitors, staff and trustees for her inspiring visit to the UK and the wonderful way in which she interacted with intellectually curious students and others who engaged with her.

PHILIP BOOTH

Editorial and Programme Director,
Institute of Economic Affairs
Professor of Insurance and Risk Management,
Cass Business School, City University
September 2012

The views expressed in this monograph are, as in all IEA publications, those of the author and not those of the Institute (which has no corporate view), its managing trustees, Academic Advisory Council members or senior staff.

SUMMARY

- Traditional economic models of how to manage environmental problems relating to renewable natural resources, such as fisheries, have tended to recommend either government regulation or privatisation and the explicit definition of property rights.
- These traditional models ignore the practical reality of natural resource management. Many communities are able to spontaneously develop their own approaches to managing such common-pool resources. In the words of Mark Pennington: '[Professor Ostrom's] book *Governing the Commons* is a superb testament to the understanding that can be gained when economists observe in close-up detail how people craft arrangements to solve problems in ways often beyond the imagination of textbook theorists.'
- In particular, communities are often able to find stable and effective ways to define the boundaries of a common-pool resource, define the rules for its use and effectively enforce those rules.
- The effective management of a natural resource often requires 'polycentric' systems of governance where various entities have some role in the process. Government may play a role in some circumstances, perhaps by providing information to

resource users or by assisting enforcement processes through court systems.

- Elinor Ostrom's work in this field, for which she won the Nobel Prize in economics in 2009, was grounded in the detailed empirical study of how communities managed common-pool resources in practice.

- It is essential that we avoid the 'panacea problem'. There is no correct way to manage common-pool resources that will always be effective. Different ways of managing resources will be appropriate in different contexts – for example within different cultures or where there are different physical characteristics of a natural resource.

- Nevertheless, there are principles that we can draw from the detailed study of the salient features of different cases to help us understand how different common-pool resources might be best managed; which rules systems and systems of organisation have the best chance of success or failure; and so on.

- Elinor Ostrom's approach has been praised by the left, who often see it as being opposed to free-market privatisation initiatives. In fact, her approach sits firmly within the classical liberal tradition of political economy. She observes communities freely choosing their own mechanisms to manage natural resource problems without government coercion or planning.

- In developing a viable approach to the management of the commons, it is important, among other things, that a resource can be clearly defined and that the rules governing the use of the resource are adapted to local conditions. This suggests that rules imposed from outside, such as by government agencies, are unlikely to be successful.

- There are important areas of natural resource management where Elinor Ostrom's ideas should be adopted to avoid environmental catastrophe. Perhaps the most obvious example relevant to the UK is in European Union fisheries policy. Here, there is one centralised model for the management of the resource that is applied right across the European Union, ignoring all the evidence about the failure of that approach.

FIGURES AND TABLE

The Future of the Commons

1 ELINOR OSTROM, COMMON-POOL RESOURCES AND THE CLASSICAL LIBERAL TRADITION

Mark Pennington

Introduction

I am very honoured to contribute this introduction to the ideas of Professor Elinor Ostrom. My own work has often drawn inspiration from her writings and it was a privilege to speak to Professor Ostrom at a lunch hosted by the IEA prior to the annual Hayek Lecture which is the subject of this occasional paper. Her sad loss, a matter of weeks on from that lecture, leaves the world without one of the most innovative social scientists of the last century.

In an introductory essay, I cannot hope to convey all of the insight and nuance that characterised Professor Ostrom's research over a period of 40 years. I aim instead to provide readers with a broad outline of her work focusing on three particular dimensions. The first and longest section sets out the core principles that underscore her analysis of common-pool resources and her argument for moving beyond the dichotomy between 'privatisation' and 'government regulation'. The second section examines the implications of Professor Ostrom's ideas for the classical liberal tradition. Towards the end of his life Hayek noted the need for a more creative appreciation of the way in which institutions of property rights might be adapted in view of emerging problems of environmental protection (Hayek, 1988). Ostrom's work has been crucial in identifying what these alternative property institutions might look like. In addition, I hope to show how some of these insights can be applied beyond the realm of resource conservation to a broader range of socio-economic questions where the case for decentralised forms of governance is often overlooked. The final section briefly sets out how Professor Ostrom's work might impact on economics as a profession.

Ostrom on incentives and the management of common-pool resources

Elinor Ostrom's Nobel Prize-winning work on the management of common-pool resources can be situated broadly within the rational-choice tradition in economic and political theory. Long before this work attracted widespread attention, she and her husband Vincent were pioneers in public choice theory, constitutional political economy and what has come to be known as the 'new institutionalism' (Aligica and Boettke, 2009). Though accepting that actors are not purely rational, that they suffer from incomplete information and various cognitive limitations, Ostrom's framework recognises that individuals are nonetheless purposeful actors who respond to incentives. Institutions shape the incentives that people face and affect the likelihood of whether they will coordinate their actions successfully or whether they will engage in negative-sum games. 'Institutions' refers both to formal and 'hard' institutions, such as the relative extent of individual, communal and state-owned property rights and a legal system which enforces these rights; and to informal or 'soft' institutions such as cultural attitudes towards promise-keeping, and preferences for long- or short-term gain.

Ostrom and the new institutionalism: rethinking institutions and incentives

Though economists have traditionally focused on the role of institutions and incentives, many analysts have approached the interrelationship between them in a simplistic way. Nowhere has this simplistic mode of thought been more entrenched than in discussion of common-pool resources. Traditionally, analysts have assumed that *all* common-pool resources suffer from the same deficient incentive structure which leads to widespread 'free-riding'. When resources exist in an unowned state, so the argument goes, no individual will have an incentive to conserve because to do so will simply leave more resources for others to take. In the absence of exclusion devices which enable people to profit personally from conservation, they will extract as much of the resource as possible up to the point of depletion. According to this view, as popularised by Garret Hardin (1968), the only way to internalise externalities and avoid the 'tragedy of the commons' is to have an external body impose a management structure over the resource. This structure can take the form of either private ownership, where exclusive rights to extract fish, timber, water, etc., are parcelled out to individual owners, or it can take the form of government ownership, where the state takes responsibility for managing the asset either through direct control or via the external imposition of rules and regulations.

Ostrom's work represents a direct challenge to this form of theorising because, while recognising that incentives matter, she argues that incentive structures are more varied and complex than conventional analysis assumes.[1] In the case of common-pool

1   The 'tragedy of the commons' should really be described as the 'tragedy of open access'. The type of scenario discussed by Hardin refers to a situation where

resources, it is *not* always the case that resources will be over-exploited. There are many instances where communities of resource users have managed to develop exclusion methods and evolve effective rules which have avoided the tragedy of the commons *without* external regulation. Examples include the management of commonly owned pastures in the Swiss Alps, the regulation of grazing and logging on commonly held meadows and forests in Japan, the sustainable management of inshore fisheries by cooperatives in the eastern United States, and the supervision of complex irrigation systems in the Valencia region of Spain (Ostrom, 1990: ch. 3).

On the other hand, there are numerous examples where attempts to impose individual property rights or government ownership and regulation have had disastrous consequences. Thus, attempts to privatise natural resources in some of the transition economies and in parts of Africa, where basic norms emphasising the protection of individual property rights do not exist, have resulted in rampant corruption and cronyism as ruling elites have sought to grab access to resources for themselves and their political and tribal allies (Van de Walle, 2001). In the case of government ownership, meanwhile, there is a whole catalogue of cases where the takeover of natural resources by government agencies has produced disastrous results. In developed nations, this includes the dismal record of centralising measures such as

---

there are *no* rules governing the use of the resource. This is a very rare situation. In practice, most common-pool resources are governed by a set of rules – but the origin of these rules differs. In some circumstances they are developed endogenously by the resource users themselves, but elsewhere they are imposed on resource users by an external governing body. The debate about the relative efficacy of internally generated versus externally imposed rules is what Ostrom highlights so well.

the European Common Fisheries Policy, which prevents fishermen either at the local or even at the national level from devising rules to limit overfishing (De Alessi, 1998). In developing nations it includes the miserable record of nationalised forests and irrigation systems where centralised management has replaced intricate and long-standing customary rules for dealing with resource scarcity and conflict (Ostrom, 1990: 23).

Though highly critical of externally imposed solutions to common-pool problems, Ostrom *does not* claim that decentralised community-based approaches are always the most appropriate institutional form. She recognises that in many cases individualised property institutions may be better placed to incentivise resource conservation and to allow greater scope for innovation than more collective structures (for example, McKean and Ostrom, 1995). Similarly, she appreciates that in some circumstances neither private nor communal management may be feasible and that there may be no alternative to relying on state regulation. The question that Ostrom sets herself is to discover what factors are most likely to result in bottom-up solutions to potential common-pool problems and what factors are likely to thwart the development of these solutions. Similarly, she aims to provide a framework that can guide decisions about when to rely on spontaneous processes of governance and when to rely on the external generation of rules. The key elements of this multilevel framework for understanding what Ostrom refers to as 'socioecological systems' and the 'design principles' to emerge from it are set out below.

Socio-ecological systems and design principles for common-pool resources

Boundaries to facilitate exclusion

A key factor affecting the likelihood of bottom-up solutions developing is the character of the resource and, in particular, the existence or otherwise of clearly defined boundaries. Exclusion mechanisms are the key to overcoming free-riding, and resource boundaries increase the capacity for those who use a resource to limit access by those living *outside* the community in question. Common-pool resources vary significantly in terms of these boundary attributes. Grazing land in a mountain valley, for example, might have clearly defined boundaries owing to the nature of the surrounding terrain, whereas open grassland on a large plateau may lack such natural markers. Similarly, inshore fisheries often have clearly defined natural boundaries, whereas offshore fisheries frequently do not.

The importance of internal rules

Though the existence of boundaries to limit access by those *outside* a community of resource users is important, it is also critical that there are rules which prevent people *within* the community concerned from appropriating too much of the resource. Successful models of resource management such as the Swiss mountain commons and the Valencia irrigation system in Spain specify clear procedures for when and how the resource can be used.

The importance of locally adapted rules

Resources vary across time and place, so no single management rule will be appropriate in all circumstances. The character of resource users also varies and this affects the capacity to overcome potential free-riding and opportunistic behaviour. *Ceteris paribus*, the smaller the population of resource users the easier it will be to detect people who are abusing the rules. Similarly, a culturally homogeneous and relatively stable community where people have strong reputational and social ties and a commitment to long-term development is less likely to invite free-riding than a more mobile community with no strong sense of local or cultural identification. Groups which possess a high degree of interpersonal trust or social capital are more likely to arrive at commonly agreed rules and to adhere to these rules than are those lacking such social capital. If they are to be successful, therefore, the rules for resource management need to reflect this sociocultural variety.

The importance of monitoring and enforcement

According to Ostrom, the most successful systems for common-pool resource management also include strong monitoring and enforcement mechanisms. In the Swiss Alpine commons, for example, village courts impose fines on those who exceed their allotted grazing rights. Even when a community exhibits strong social cohesion there will be a tendency for people to break the rules if there are no rewards for upholding and no penalties for breaking them. In addition, communities where the population has a moral commitment to the rules in operation are likely to fare better in securing enforcement than those lacking a moral identification with the relevant rules. When people derive a personal sense of utility from knowing that 'right has been done' they are more likely to enforce rules, even when this may be relatively costly to themselves, than when actors lack a strong sense of right and wrong (on the significance of preferences for rule enforcement, see Gaus, 2011).

Dispute resolution

The existence of clear and well-established procedures for dispute resolution may also increase the scope for the decentralised resolution of common-pool resource problems. Even in relatively homogeneous and stable communities disagreements over the correct interpretation of user rights are likely to arise. Communities with well-developed and transparent court systems tend to generate more sustainable forms of common-pool resource management. The Valencia region of Spain is, for example, prone to frequent conflicts and disputes over water access, owing to the often erratic pattern of rainfall and river replenishment. Nonetheless, the holding of regular tribunals and court proceedings has provided a context for speedy and efficient dispute resolution and helped to sustain effective management of the irrigation system over several centuries, notwithstanding rapid social and technological change. In the absence of such systems, incentives to avoid a 'scramble for resources' are much weaker and a tragedy of the commons is likely to assert itself.

Interaction between systems of rules

A final and often fundamental factor affecting the character of common-pool problems is the constitutional relationship between different layers of rule-making. A key finding of Ostrom's work is that effective rules are more likely to arise in situations where those who have an immediate stake in overcoming common-pool resource problems are actively involved in shaping and enforcing governance arrangements. When communities make rules for themselves they have strong incentives to make the rules work and to learn from their mistakes. When locally established rules and property rights are not respected by higher tiers of governance, and especially when higher authorities respond to the demands of external interest groups to allow access to a resource base, then common-pool resource systems may be highly fragile. This has been a particular problem in many parts of the developing world, where local customary rights to use forests and other resources have often been overridden by national governments responding to the demands of either domestic or international business interests in resource-extraction industries. Similarly, in contexts where central authorities assume responsibility for determining most of the rules that govern the use of resources, there will be a diminished incentive for those involved at the local level to find ways of devising their own governance arrangements.

Action situations and institutional implications

All the factors listed above affect the incentive structure that faces participants in the context of specific common-pool resources, and these incentives constitute what Ostrom calls particular 'action situations'.

The most important point to emerge from Ostrom's account of socio-ecological systems is that there are many 'action situations' where decentralised community governance can work well. Specifically, when there are clear boundaries to a resource; where a community has high levels of interpersonal trust or social capital; where there are procedures for resolving disputes; and where the community concerned has sufficient decision-making autonomy to create, monitor and enforce its own rules and to exclude outsiders, then incentives can operate to avoid the 'tragedy of the commons'. In these 'common property regimes' resources are *exclusive* to a particular community rather than being 'publicly owned', but, instead of parcelling out the assets to individuals, the exclusive owner is a decentralised communal unit (McKean and Ostrom, 1995: 6).

Many of the most successful models of commons management that Ostrom cites are 'mixed regimes' including elements of individual and common property. In the Swiss Alps, for example, farmers have individually owned plots for the growing of vegetables, fruit trees and hay for winter fodder, but the summer meadows, forests, irrigation systems and the paths and roads connecting individually and communally owned plots are managed by a village-level association (Ostrom, 1990: 61–5). Such arrangements work particularly well where the scale of the resource or common-pool resource problem makes it too difficult to create purely individual private property rights or where there may be cultural hostility to the concept of individual property.

In other contexts, however, the creation of individual private property rights may indeed prove more effective. When, for example, there are clear boundaries to a resource but where the community is highly mobile and culturally heterogeneous, then incentives may be insufficient to create and enforce effective communal rules. Individual private property rights work well precisely because they minimise the need for agreement between resource users. Actors, whether individuals or corporate bodies, can use a resource as they see fit without requiring permission from a superior hierarchy or a committee of their neighbours. At the same time, *provided the property rights are reasonably well defined* and that there are effective courts and dispute resolution procedures in place, individual private property rights operate to internalise costs and benefits – the property owner reaps the potential rewards from conserving a resource and suffers losses for failing to maintain it. A significant body of empirical work confirms that for a wide range of resources, including forests, minerals, oyster beds and some inshore fisheries, private property institutions work to promote highly sustainable management practices (for a summary of this evidence, see De Alessi, 2003).

Government ownership or regulation is more likely to be relatively more effective in contexts where none of the above factors is present and hence where there is little or no scope for either community governance or individual private property arrangements to develop. This is most likely to be so when there are no clear boundaries to the resource, where there is a large-scale and highly mobile and diverse population of resource users; this leads to a situation where the transaction costs of arriving at and enforcing decentralised solutions may be prohibitive. Regional and international problems of trans-boundary air pollution and the problem of anthropogenic climate change seem to be the most obvious candidates that fall into this category, where there may be no alternative but to rely on centrally imposed rules to incentivise changes in behaviour.

The presumption against central planning

Though Ostrom recognises that there may be a class of resource management problems that require some form of external, centrally imposed regulation, it is important to recognise that there is a strong presumption *against* relying on such methods, even in situations where community governance or individual property solutions have *not yet* developed. There are a number of reasons underlying this presumption against central planning.

The first is that central regulatory authorities often lack

knowledge about the specific character of the assets to be managed and the nature of the incentives facing resource users. Effective regulation requires that those devising regulatory rules have sufficient knowledge of on-the-ground incentives in order to create and to enforce rules which can change those incentives in a manner encouraging conservation. More often than not central regulators lack this kind of knowledge. Distant bureaucrats may not be aware of the physical characteristics of the resource in question – whether there are potential resource boundaries, subtle variations in climatic patterns, etc. – which should affect the character of the rules chosen. Some of this information might be gathered by a government department if sufficient resources could be devoted to this task, but this may prove more costly than relying on the knowledge of those who are actually resident on site.

There are, however, other forms of knowledge, which *even in principle* central regulators will be unlikely to be able to access. Knowledge of the cultural norms and values that structure the way in which people perceive and respond to resource-management issues and how these values evolve is embedded in the minds and everyday culture of those who inhabit the communities concerned. This is what Hayek (1945) refers to as knowledge of the 'circumstances of time and place', which is often tacit and which cannot be expressed in verbal statements or regulatory statutes. As a consequence, it is unlikely that external regulators will understand enough about the specific incentives that face resource users to be able to devise an effective set of rules. In addition, bureaucrats in central agencies typically lack a sufficient personal stake to manage assets effectively. Since their status and remuneration are largely detached from success at the local level they are prone to respond more to their own budgetary imperatives and to the demands of interest groups that are often seeking to redistribute property rights rather than engage in mutually beneficial contracts with the communities concerned.

A second reason to avoid immediate recourse to central regulation is that the very act of regulating from the centre undermines the incentive for resource users themselves to devise an appropriate set of rules. When the state takes over responsibility for managing an asset, individuals and groups that do not already have their own institutions in place will simply wait for the government to handle their problems for them. As Ostrom (1990: 213) puts it: 'if someone else agrees to pay the costs of supplying new institutions then it is difficult to avoid the temptation to free-ride'. Under these conditions there is little incentive for local actors to find ways of using their own culturally specific knowledge to build up effective governance procedures from below. This 'crowding out' effect reduces the capacity of communities to develop mechanisms needed to monitor free-riding behaviour and to create the social capital required to overcome resource conservation dilemmas. Indeed, if the community itself developed institutions to deal with resource management when state systems existed, there would be the potential for conflict between the two sets of institutions (state and community) and huge uncertainty about how such conflicts might be resolved. This kind of uncertainty, in many situations, can lead to substantial welfare losses.

Even relatively large-scale collective-action problems are more likely to be solved when the necessary institutions are developed *from below*. Many of the most successful cases of river catchment supervision, for example, have occurred when relatively small groups of water users at the level of individual river basins have first created localised associations to manage access. The creation of these institutions at the most decentralised level has then enabled them to build further institutions to devise and enforce rules and to link with other communities at the *inter-basin* level in order to manage the catchments as a whole. By contrast, when water users have lobbied regional governments to have a single agency take over management of the resource, this has frequently led to the capture of such agencies by bureaucrats and external rent-seeking interest groups aiming to redistribute resources rather than address the underlying resource scarcity (Ostrom, 1990: ch. 5).

A final and perhaps most important reason to presume against central planning is that it removes the scope for people to learn how to address common-pool resource problems more effectively. Decision-making over natural resources does not start from a situation where the most effective institutional form for managing the resource is 'given' in advance. On the contrary, knowledge of the kinds of rules, institutions and technologies that can be combined in order to internalise externalities needs to be discovered through a dynamic, evolutionary process of trial-and-error learning (Ostrom, 2005). There is, therefore, a strong case for relying on polycentric rather than monocentric structures of governance. Very few environmental goods are completely indivisible in supply – most are territorial and their supply can vary within countries and between regions and much smaller localities. In principle, therefore, such goods are suited to a process of 'parallel adaptation' where a variety of institutional devices compete and where people can copy and adapt the most successful models to their own circumstances (ibid.). Such a process will not secure an 'optimal solution', but by allowing for trial and error evolution it increases the chance of discovering beneficial institutions. Should there be only one rule-making body, then any errors are likely to have systemic effects. In a polycentric order, mistakes, though inevitable, are confined to the resource owners in question. Adaptation is also speedier than in a more unitary equivalent – actors can learn from and imitate the most successful models adopted by their neighbours without waiting for approval from some overarching authority or majority.

The role of the state in environmental resource management – what we can learn from Ostrom

None of the above should be taken to imply that Ostrom's framework rules out a role for the state. More specifically, states can play a useful role if they facilitate development of the dispute resolution procedures and ensure legal recognition for the local property rights structures which are a key ingredient in creating incentives to overcome free-riding. States might also serve a useful function by spreading information about new scientific or technical knowledge pertinent to the management of a particular resource – though this knowledge should be used in conjunction with, rather than replacing, the more localised and culturally specific know-how that resides at the community level. Governments might also be involved in the ownership or regulation of some common-pool resources where the transaction costs of securing common or private property arrangements are too high. In general, though, so long as the resources in question are at least partially divisible, this activity should be confined to municipal or local government structures which have the autonomy to raise their own revenues and create their own locally adapted rules.

Federal or polycentric political structures provide a laboratory for experiments in institutional design which can be spread by a process of trial-and-error learning across jurisdictions. *What should be avoided, wherever possible, is a unitary model of ownership and/or control by a central government agency.*

In the context of many developing countries, attention to the design principles set out above would represent a marked reversal of policy trends in the post-colonial era. The tendency to perceive nationalisation as a more efficient and modern form of management (a tendency often encouraged by external aid agencies) has been particularly unfortunate. In Nepal, for example, nationalisation of forestry in the post-war era resulted in widespread resource depletion as people no longer subject to communal rules engaged in free-riding behaviour while national bureaucrats had few incentives to monitor the enforcement of officially imposed rules and regulations. Only recently have governments begun to see the error of this approach and to give more autonomy to communities and individuals, but there is still a deep reluctance to grant full autonomy to localised governance structures (Ostrom, 1990: 178).

More generally, governments in developing nations need to recognise and protect the property rights of their own people, and international aid agencies need to stop funding those who refuse to respect these rights. When governments have been attentive to the enforcement of communal rights, as for example in New Guinea, then communities can be well placed to manage assets, even in negotiations with large external agents, such as oil and timber companies. Many of the problems associated with deforestation and pollution have not resulted from a failure of markets or of community governance but from central government actions which have directly undermined local property rights systems. On the one hand, governments in places from Brazil to Nigeria have encouraged excessive resource extraction by directly subsidising road building, logging and oil exploration in highly sensitive areas. On the other hand, they have failed to protect the property rights of local people who have come into contact with extractive industries as a result of these subsidies and in some cases have been complicit in expropriating these very rights (Anderson and Leal, 2001: ch. 11).

Developed countries, too, have much to learn from Ostrom's approach. Many resources could be managed more effectively through a decentralised mix of communal and private property structures with the state acting in a facilitative role. Instead, governments often have more-or-less exclusive control of many environmental resources. In Britain, for example, it is disappointing that the recent report by the Independent Panel on Forestry has recommended retaining the Forestry Commission's assets in public ownership with an increased commitment to central funding. Forestry provides a fairly clear-cut case where enforceable boundaries can enable either private or community-based owners to manage access and craft rules to balance the competing demands for commercial extraction, recreational access and conservation.

At the EU level, the Common Fisheries Policy is desperately in need of an Ostrom-inspired reform agenda. While there are clear logistical difficulties in trying to enforce individual private property rights and even communal property rules over offshore fisheries, it is manifestly inappropriate for a fishery from the Baltic to the Mediterranean to be managed as if it were a single resource. At the very least, there is a strong case for the repatriation of fisheries management to nation-states with the European

Union providing a dispute resolution function between member states. Ideally, however, there should be still further decentralisation of decision-making, rebuilding the cooperative fishermen's associations that used to manage local fisheries but which have been systematically undermined by EU legislation.

Ostrom and the classical liberal tradition

Throughout her career Elinor Ostrom was keen to avoid crude ideological labelling, and the title of her Hayek Lecture, 'Beyond market failure and government regulation', confirms a long-standing determination to chart an intellectual course avoiding conventional left versus right confrontations on the relative efficacy of free markets and state regulation. Nonetheless, there is a good deal within the intellectual space that Ostrom carves out that is thoroughly at one with the basic insights of classical liberal political economy.

At root, Ostrom's arguments showing the frequent, though not universal, efficacy of decentralised governance are an application of what has come to be known as 'robust political economy' (on this, see Pennington, 2011; Leeson and Subrick, 2006). Robust political economy analysis evaluates institutions according to their capacity to cope with two human imperfections. On the one hand, the problem of limited knowledge – the fact that even the most intelligent actors are relatively ignorant of their surroundings and are prone to make mistakes. And, on the other hand, the problem of limited benevolence – the fact that people are often unwilling to contribute to the good of their fellows unless they are able to gain some personal benefit from doing so.

The classical liberal case for a regime based on strong

protection of private property, extensive reliance on civil society and voluntary association, and a limited and decentralised form of government is based on the view that the dispersed (though unequal) ownership of property in a market system is more robust in the face of these imperfections than more centralised alternatives. By decentralising decision-making to many different individuals and organisations, it facilitates a greater level of experimentation than more state-centric regimes, allowing for evolutionary learning while minimising the impact of inevitable mistakes. At the same time, it provides better incentives for people by allowing them to reap the rewards of decisions which benefit their fellows and to bear penalties for failing to do so. Ostrom's arguments are based on the similar contention that decentralised forms of governance are better placed to enable trial-and-error discovery of the rules needed to overcome common-pool resource problems and to provide incentives for those most affected by such rules to make them work.

Within this context, it is important to confront a myth, propagated by some ill-informed opinion, that Ostrom's research somehow constitutes a refutation of 'neoliberal' economics and its arguments in favour of privately owned and decentralised property regimes. Two examples of this opinion are set out below.

Writing in the *Guardian* in October 2009, Kevin Gallagher claimed that: 'In a nutshell, Ostrom won the Nobel Prize for showing that privatising natural resources is not the route to halting environmental degradation' (*Guardian*, 13 October 2009).

Similarly, the Nobel laureate Joseph Stiglitz was quoted in the *New York Times* saying: 'Conservatives use the Tragedy of the Commons to argue for property rights ... What Ostrom has demonstrated is the existence of social control mechanisms that regulate the use of the commons without having to resort to property rights' (*New York Times*, 12 October 2009).

Gallagher's journalistic lack of acquaintance with Ostrom's work is sloppy though perhaps understandable, but Stiglitz's statement is frankly reprehensible. At no point does Ostrom claim that commons problems can be addressed 'without having to resort to property rights'. Property rights and the ability to exclude outsiders are fundamental to the common property regimes which Ostrom believes provide an alternative to parcelling out resources either to discrete individuals or to public ownership. Similarly, at no point does Ostrom refute the case for private ownership per se, though she questions the wisdom of external agents imposing *individualised* property rights in communities which have evolved effective common property regimes. Common property regimes are themselves, according to Ostrom, a form of exclusive private property – it is just that private property rights should not always be equated with *individual* property rights. In the words of Ostrom and her co-author Margaret McKean, '*It is crucial to recognise that common property is shared private property ...*'

They proceed:

> Common property regimes are a way of privatising the
> rights to something without dividing it into pieces ...
> Historically common property regimes have evolved in
> places where the demand on a resource is too great to
> tolerate open access, so property rights have to be created,
> but some other factor makes it impossible or undesirable to
> parcel the resource itself. (McKean and Ostrom, 1995: 6)

Few would suggest that the condominium associations and private (sometimes gated) communities that have spread rapidly over recent years across the USA and East Asia as bottom-up alternatives to the municipal provision of collective goods are *not* a form of 'privatisation'. Indeed, many leftist/social democratic critics have condemned them as such (McKenzie, 1996). These are, however, precisely the type of 'mixed' property arrangements that Ostrom thinks can and should be used much more widely. Residents have individual property rights to their houses but must submit to common regulations developed by the cooperative association in order to maintain aesthetic standards, control new development and ensure contributions to goods such as parks, roads and street lighting. It is, therefore, a mistake common to simplistic versions of 'left-wing' and 'right-wing' thinking to equate the case for privatisation with individual ownership. Condominiums and private communities provide a clear case of private – though not necessarily individual – ownership.

At the core of Ostrom's work is the insight that many, though not all, of the free-rider and collective-good problems that are usually presented as requiring external regulation may be better addressed by relying on the ingenuity of those most affected by them to devise an appropriate set of rules. This is an insight that is close to the heart of the classical liberal tradition and which has prompted a new generation of scholars to catalogue cases where we observe the formation of rules without the exercise of external authority.

The development and enforcement of the rules governing international commercial contracts provide an important case in point. A well-functioning market with effective rules against fraud and crooked dealing is an example of a collective good – it is in the collective interests of all participants in the market that such rules exist, but it may not be in the specific interests of individual participants to uphold these rules because each actor may gain a personal advantage by engaging in fraud and opportunism. Seen through the lens of market failure, or, to be more precise, 'decentralisation failure', analysis, international trade should be a particularly unpromising area for there to be any kind of order because there is no formal state or state-like authority at the global level to enforce the terms of international contracts.

As Leeson (2008) has shown, however, notwithstanding the absence of external authority, an effective system of decentralised rule enforcement via private arbitration has evolved to facilitate a massive expansion in trans-border trade. There are currently over a hundred international arbitration agencies across the world, including organisations such as the International Chamber of Commerce and the London Court of Arbitration, and 90 per cent or more of international contracts contain relevant arbitration clauses. Willingness to sign up to private arbitration sends out a signal that the party concerned is unlikely to renege on a deal. Those who refuse to be bound by the terms of arbitration, meanwhile, are unlikely to find partners with whom to trade. Abuses occur within this system, but in a context where there are multiple organisations needing periodically to cooperate with others there are powerful incentives for trans-boundary actors to develop a reputation for good conduct and to monitor enforcement of the rules.

The case of international private arbitration is an 'Ostromesque' example where those actors affected most by regulation have incentives to develop and to participate actively in the enforcement of effective governance institutions. It is, however, precisely these incentives which have been progressively undermined in areas such as the regulation of money and banking. Prior to the advent of regulatory institutions such as the US Federal

Reserve, individual banks and banking associations competed for funds on the basis of reputation and a system of 'private law'. In the absence of state-supported deposit insurance, private lending institutions had to attract depositors by, for example, ensuring the acceptability of the currencies they issued, thus limiting the potential for 'bank runs' to insolvent institutions, and monitoring the character of lending practices in member associations. Depositors, meanwhile, had strong incentives to seek out those institutions with the most secure reputation because a failure to invest with a sound bank could risk their entire investment. The presence of these incentives was by no means sufficient to eradicate financial crises and panics over institutional solvency, but they did provide a context where the effects of any abuse of trust could be confined to a relatively small sphere (White, 1984; Timberlake, 1993).

The advent of a government-regulated banking industry has, over time, transformed this nexus of incentives. With centralised government institutions assuming more and more responsibility for the integrity of the financial system, individual banks no longer have a strong incentive to develop a reputation for best practice. Instead of competing for depositors on the basis of probity, banking institutions increasingly seek ways to *avoid* government regulations – safe in the knowledge that should their practices prompt a 'bank run', they will be 'bailed out' by the state. On the demand side, the provision of state-financed deposit insurance has reduced the incentive for depositors to seek out the most trustworthy institutions. With the state committed implicitly or explicitly to bailing out banks, there is little reason for people to incur the costs of seeking out best-practice institutions. From a classical liberal perspective, it is this incentive structure which has pervaded financial markets for much of the last 100 years, under-mining the integrity of markets and increasing the possibility of 'systemic failure'.

The above argument does not deny a potential role for the state in the regulation of financial markets. Indeed, with the state so heavily involved in the current operation of these markets, it is difficult to see how *any* programme of reform could eschew government action in its entirety. What it does suggest, however, is the need for an Ostrom-inspired willingness to appreciate how layers of centrally imposed regulation can undermine incentives for what might be a more effective set of bottom-up rules. This level of sophistication is sadly lacking in contemporary commentaries, which assert that 'markets have failed' and that central governments should regulate even more intrusively in order to avoid future financial crises.

Conclusion: Ostrom and the need for a new economics

Elinor Ostrom was a political scientist by training, but like many economists her work recognises the importance of institutions and the role they play in shaping incentives. Ostrom's analysis, however, should be seen as a call to economists to move beyond the sterile 'blackboard' analysis of 'markets' and 'government' to look at how *actual* institutions operate *on the ground.* Though she was keen to use aggregate statistical studies when appropriate, Ostrom's research also demonstrates the great value of detailed case studies. Her book *Governing the Commons* is a superb testament to the understanding that can be gained when economists observe in close-up detail how people craft arrangements to solve problems in ways often beyond the imagination of textbook theorists. More often than not, this kind of appreciation is excluded when theorists develop abstract models of economic incentives and confine empirical work to the manipulation of large-scale data sets which miss out on the causal role played by fine-grained institutional detail. Sadly, the appreciation of case-study work has all but disappeared from mainstream empirical economics with its erroneous belief in the superior scientific status of large-scale quantitative modelling.

Ostrom's case-study work follows the example set by another Nobel laureate and founder of the 'new institutionalism' – Ronald Coase. Among his many achievements Coase showed that lighthouses, which many economists had theorised as a non-excludable collective good and thus unlikely to be supplied privately, were in fact historically supplied by largely private means (Coase, 1974; see also Barnett and Block, 2007). Economists had typically assumed that vessels could benefit from lighthouse services irrespective of payment when, in fact, lighthouses were often owned by harbour companies with fees charged on entrance to port. Nonetheless, it is still common to find economists, who would never dream of 'getting their hands dirty' with such case-study work, continuing to assert that lighthouses cannot be supplied on a private basis. One can only hope that, in years to come, economists will not be insisting that externally imposed privatisation through individualisation of property rights or government control provide the only ways to escape the tragedy of the commons. Elinor Ostrom's work must result in a renewed appreciation of the role of case studies in economics and must continue to receive the credit it so richly deserves.

References

Aligica, P. D. and P. Boettke (2009), *Challenging Institutional Analysis and Development: The Bloomington School*, London: Routledge.

Anderson, T. and D. Leal (2001), *Free Market Environmentalism*, New York: Palgrave.

Barnett, W. and W. Block (2007), 'Coase and Van Zandt on lighthouses', *Public Finance Review*, 35(6): 711–33.

Coase, R. (1974), 'The lighthouse in economics', *Journal of Law and Economics*, 17(2): 357–76.

De Alessi, L. (2003), 'Gains from private property: the empirical evidence', in T. Anderson and F. McChesney (eds), *Property Rights: Cooperation, Conflict and Law*, Princeton, NJ: Princeton University Press.

De Alessi, M. (1998), *Fishing for Solutions*, London: Institute of Economic Affairs.

Gaus, G. (2011), *The Order of Public Reason*, Cambridge: Cambridge University Press.

Hardin, G. (1968), 'The tragedy of the commons', *Science*, 162: 1243–8.

Hayek, F. A. (1945), 'The use of knowledge in society', *American Economic Review*, 35(4): 519–30.

Hayek, F. A. (1988), *The Fatal Conceit*, London: Routledge.

Leeson, P. (2008), 'How important is state enforcement for trade?', *American Law and Economics Review*, 10(1): 61–89.

Leeson, P. and R. Subrick (2006), 'Robust political economy', *Review of Austrian Economics*, 19: 107–11.

McKean, M. and E. Ostrom (1995), 'Common property regimes in the forest: just a relic from the past?', *Unasylva*, 46(180): 3–15.

McKenzie, E. (1996), *Privatopia*, New Haven, CT: Yale University Press.

Ostrom, E. (1990), *Governing the Commons: The Evolution of Institutions for Collective Action*, Cambridge: Cambridge University Press.

Ostrom, E. (2005), *Understanding Institutional Diversity*, Princeton, NJ: Princeton University Press.

Pennington, M. (2011), *Robust Political Economy: Classical Liberalism and the Future of Public Policy*, Cheltenham: Edward Elgar.

Timberlake, R. (1993), *Monetary Policy in the United States*, Chicago, IL: University of Chicago Press.

Van de Walle, N. (2001), *African Economies and the Politics of Permanent Crisis*, Cambridge: Cambridge University Press.

White, L. (1984), *Free Banking in Britain*, Cambridge: Cambridge University Press.

2 ELINOR OSTROM'S LIFE AND WORK

Vlad Tarko

The life of Elinor Ostrom[1]

Elinor Ostrom was born in 1933 and grew up in the midst of the Great Depression in Los Angeles. When her parents divorced, she remained with her mother and they lived in relatively poor conditions, having to grow their own food in their backyard garden. She went to Beverly Hills High School, across the street from her house. 'I'm very grateful for that opportunity,' she later recalled, 'because 90 per cent of the kids who went to Beverly Hills High School went on to college. I don't think I would have gone to college if not for being in that environment.' She graduated from the University of California, Los Angeles (UCLA), in 1954 with a major in political science, after which she married her first husband, Charles Scott, a classmate. They moved to Boston, where she worked as assistant personnel manager at a law firm, while Charles went to Harvard's law school. 'Basically I put my husband through law school,' she recalled. They divorced after three years and she returned to UCLA to work in the personnel office.

After deciding to take a course in public administration, more or less as a hobby, she became so fascinated with the subject

---

1   Herald-Times (2009); Zagorski (2006).

matter that she ended up getting a master's degree and a PhD in political science, which was quite unusual for a woman at the time. Her dissertation was about water management in California, setting her on course for what would become a lifelong study of how communities self-organise in response to various challenges. In 1963 she married fellow political scientist Vincent Ostrom and the couple moved to Bloomington a year later. There, at Indiana University, they started the Workshop in Political Theory and Policy Analysis in 1973, after having set up a series of informal weekly meetings in 1969.

The workshop became a major interdisciplinary research centre, and a key actor in the rise of new institutionalism and in public choice economics. Over the years, the Ostroms received offers from Harvard and Duke, but they decided to remain at Indiana: 'my sense has been that you don't build something like this [workshop] and just move it', explained Elinor Ostrom. 'Part of the staff are not movable. They understand the enterprise and they make a difference. We've had faculty colleagues who were just great. We have a team and you don't pick up and move a whole team.' When she won the Nobel Prize in Economics in 2009, she donated the money to the workshop, saying that the research honoured by the prize had been a collective effort. She died of cancer in 2012, followed by her husband just two weeks later. As Steve Horwitz put it: 'you know how much two people loved each other when one literally cannot live without the other'.

Elinor Ostrom's intellectual contributions

Elinor Ostrom's work, as part of the Bloomington school of institutionalism and public choice, can be seen as advancing fundamental economic theory with the mindset of a political scientist. It can be said that the standard economic approach to institutions, as best illustrated by 'law and economics' (Harrison, 1995; Friedman, 2000), usually assumes that the task of the economist is to devise the optimal set of institutions for achieving a maximum amount of economic efficiency, and that the standard public choice model explores the political barriers to achieving these optimal institutions in practice.[2] The standard political science approach, on the other hand, starts from a very different, and more relativistic, perspective: the realisation that people generally have important disagreements with respect to what constitutes the 'proper function' of the social system in general and of the government in particular. Economic efficiency is just one possible social goal among many, and most people would disagree that it is a goal that trumps all others. Other social goals, such as fairness, stability, social peace, voice and inclusivity, liberty, long-term resilience and adaptability, are often considered as important if not more important than economic efficiency. As such, the political scientist sets for himself or herself a much more difficult theoretical task: to explore the social-political mechanisms by which this diversity of views somehow coalesces into social order, and the reasons why the legitimacy of the existing social order, in part or in total, can break down, leading to forms of social change that can manifest themselves in various ways from gradual reform to revolution.[3]

The Bloomington school's most important contribution to economic theory has been to create a framework for institutional

---

2   Olson (1965); Mueller (1979); Buchanan et al. (1980); Tullock et al. (2002); Tullock (2005); Caplan (2008).

3   Giugni et al. (1999); Tilly (2003); Goodwin and Tilly (2006); Gaus (2011).

Figure 1   The Institutional Analysis and Development (IAD) framework

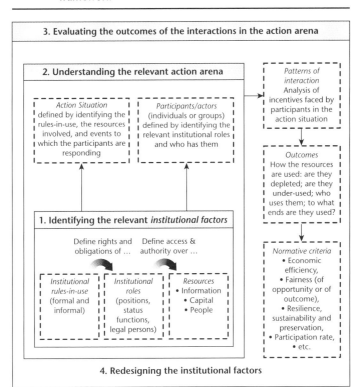

analysis and development (known for short as the 'IAD framework', Figure 1). This includes an ability to deal with this heterogeneity of normative perspectives. They have done this not by starting from scratch, but by expanding the theory of public choice within the context of new institutionalism (Ostrom and Ostrom, 2004). As such, as Aligica and Boettke (2009) note, the

Bloomington school 'is an attempt to contribute to a "revolution" in the social sciences' and 'has found itself in the middle of the major social sciences debates of the twentieth century and, at the same time, has tried to transcend them by presenting itself as a comment and an extension of a 500-year-old intellectual tradition' going back to Hobbes, a tradition preoccupied with 'the relation between spontaneous dynamics of social order, and rule-guided behavior and rule systems' (ibid.: 99, 101).

This '500-year-old intellectual tradition' is concerned with explaining social order. The Ostroms' approach to the matter focuses on institutions: i.e. on the formal and informal rules that govern human behaviour and on the mechanisms for creating and changing those rules. As a consequence of such rules, individuals are assigned, in different contexts, certain institutional roles (positions or functions) which come with specific rights and obligations. Importantly, these contexts and the roles within them are *symbolic in nature*, e.g. a border can be just a line on the ground or on a map and not an actual wall physically preventing movement, and a president is an institutional function obtained thanks to reputation and coalition-building skills and not due to being the physically strongest person (Henrich and Gil-White, 2001; Tomasello, 2009). This symbolic aspect of social rules and norms, and the assignment of institutional roles that follows from rules and norms, generates the complexity, as well as the cultural and institutional diversity, of human societies. The challenge for the social scientist is then to model and understand this complexity and variety, and the IAD framework presents itself as a comprehensive solution to this challenge (Ostrom, 2005).

The key idea of the Ostroms' institutionalism is to understand a society as a structure of interconnected and/or nested 'action arenas' and 'action situations' (see Figure 1). The complexity results from the fact that the same person may be acting in different action arenas at the same time (i.e. have more than just one institutional position, such as being both a business owner and the friend of a politician), and from the fact that decisions in one action arena take precedence over and constrain what happens in another (for example, the decision of a government official can overrule the private interactions among citizens). Importantly, this way of structuring social phenomena into inter-acting action arenas allows the researcher to focus on just one simplified problem at a time, and, when necessary, to expand the perspective to include all the relevant details from associated action arenas without being overwhelmed by the complexity of the web of social rules and norms. Moreover, this approach allows one to engage in both purely descriptive research (i.e. simply trying to understand from an outside vantage point the forces involved in the process of social change and to understand what kinds of outcomes different types of social arrangements tend to generate; Ostrom, 2008) and in normative analysis (in which one argues from a particular normative perspective in favour of the adoption of a specific change of institutions and rules).

From a simple and general perspective, we can consider four important nested action arenas: the *operational* level (the set of rules about everyday activities, directly involving the use of various resources); the *collective choice* level (the set of rules about how to change the operational rules); the *constitutional* level (the set of rules about how to change the collective choice rules and about who occupies certain key positions at the collective choice level); and the *meta-constitutional* level (constituted by moral intuitions, social norms and traditions that determine what kinds of rules at the lower levels are seen and accepted as 'legitimate'). One can see that basic economics, public choice, political science and the sociology and economics of culture become special cases of this institutionalist approach. Basic economic analysis, both micro and macro, happens at the operational level as a consequence of a particular 'given' set of rules. Public choice theory and political science, focusing on phenomena such as rent-seeking and regulatory capture (that is, special interests lobbying for rules that benefit them; Olson, 1965; Tullock, 2005), and on the impact of different voting systems (Buchanan and Tullock, 1999 [1962]; Mueller, 1979), describe the interaction between the collective choice level and the operational level. Constitutional public choice (Buchanan and Brennan, 2000 [1985]; Ostrom, 1997) analyses the way in which constitutions can effectively constrain the collective choice level and the way in which incentives at the operational level bubble up all the way to the constitutional level, creating challenges to the rule of law. Finally, the sociology and economics of culture explore the impact of the meta-constitutional level upon the lower levels, sometimes creating challenges for the adoption of better institutions and, at other times, preventing overly rushed moves in a wrong direction.[4]

As one of the leading figures of the Workshop in Political Theory and Policy Analysis, Elinor Ostrom has been at the centre of these developments, but perhaps her most important contribution was to bring to the table a strong empirical focus. While Vincent Ostrom, who was responsible for some of the most important Bloomington school theoretical developments, such as the emphasis on polycentricity, was not a complete stranger

---

4   Sperber (1996); Boettke (2001 [1996]); Ostrom (2000); Richerson and Boyd (2005); Boettke et al. (2008).

to empirical analysis himself (McGinnis and Ostrom, 2011), the empirical research that Elinor Ostrom did and organised was quite extraordinary in scope, depth and significance. Apart from research in the USA on both urban areas (for example, comparative research on police organisation in small and large departments in Indianapolis, Chicago and St Louis) and rural areas (for example, irrigation arrangements and 'water wars' in 1950s California and fisheries in Maine), her research interests in irrigation arrangements, fisheries and forest management took her around the world to countries as diverse as Nigeria, Nepal, Indonesia, the Philippines, Japan, Bolivia, Australia, Mexico, Spain, Poland, Switzerland and Sweden. This research has created a large database of case studies, organised in a manner that facilitates comparison thanks to the IAD framework. As Elinor Ostrom has often emphasised, owing to the complexity of the subject matter (there are many relevant variables that can influence the outcome), in order to be able to come up with reliable conclusions and policy recommendations, it is necessary to study a large number of diverse cases. However, the necessity of studying so many cases creates the challenge of coming up with a general enough theoretical framework to facilitate the comparison between different cases. One has to analyse the same variables in all cases, but relevant variables cannot be left out.

There have been several *empirical* results of this research programme so far. It has turned on its head some of the conventional wisdom about metropolitan administrative organisation, with regard to the supposed efficiency of centralised administration: 'The presumption that economies of scale were prevalent was wrong; the presumption that you needed a single police department was wrong; and the presumption that individual departments wouldn't be smart enough to work out ways of coordinating is wrong ... For patrolling, if you don't know the neighborhood, you can't spot the early signs of problems, and if you have five or six layers of supervision, the police chief doesn't know what's occurring on the street' (Elinor Ostrom, cited in Zagorski, 2006: 19222).

Secondly, conventional wisdom about important ecological matters has also been overturned, especially with regard to the supposed inability of communities to self-organise to create collective rules for punishing free-riders on common-pool resources. It was demonstrated that the tragedy of the commons could be avoided through such self-organisation and that universal 'panaceas' that ignore the relevant distinctions between different situations were very damaging. The other major contribution has been to discover the set of collective choice arrangements and rules ('design principles') that tend to facilitate a long-term productive relationship of a community with its environment, including its ability to respond effectively to unexpected challenges and difficulties (Ostrom, 1990, 2005). In her Hayek Memorial Lecture, Elinor Ostrom expands on these design principles and briefly explains why they work. She uses the concept of a 'socio-ecological system' (or SES for short), which is simply a concise way of referring to the connection between a community and its natural environment.

What is clear, however, is that the design principles preclude an approach to political economy that simply proposes blueprint political solutions or forms of organisation that ignore the forms of organisation that evolve within society itself, often for very good reason.

Understanding public goods and common-pool resources

Apart from the creation of the IAD framework, the most important *theoretical* contributions to economics of this empirical work have been to expand the economic theory of public goods and common-pool resources; to expand basic consumer theory by creating the theory of 'co-production'; and to better understand the importance of polycentricity. A brief explanation of these ideas is useful to help an understanding of the background of Elinor Ostrom's Hayek Memorial Lecture.

Economists often classify goods and services based on two criteria: the ease with which the producer can exclude free-riders (people who consume the good or service without paying), and the extent to which consumption by one user subtracts from the availability of the good or service for other people (how 'rivalrous' the good or service is). Based on these criteria, we have four basic types of possible goods (Table 1). If free-riding is not prevented, the good or service tends to be under-produced because most producers do not act purely out of charity and producers will not get compensated for its production. However, if consumption subtracts from the availability of the resource, free-riding also tends to deplete (destroy) the resource because most people correctly understand that, even if they themselves abstain from using the resource, the depletion will still not be stopped as others (the free-riders) will deplete it anyway (so there is no point in abstaining oneself). In other words, public goods tend to be under-produced, and common-pool resources tend to be both under-produced and over-consumed.

Table 1 **Types of goods**

		Excludability of free-riders	
		Easy	Hard
Rivalry/ subtractability of consumption	Large	Private good	Common-pool resource
	Small	Club good	Public good

The classic solution to the public goods problem has been to use taxes to pay for public goods, thus adjusting their supply level upwards (presumably towards the optimum). The classic solution to the 'tragedy of the commons' problem, provided by Hardin (1968), has been to transform the resource into a private good (either by privatising it or by turning it into government property with proper monitoring).

One of the main reasons for which Elinor Ostrom received her Nobel Prize is the discovery that these classic solutions are not the only possible ones. What Ostrom discovered in her empirical studies is that, despite what economists have thought, communities often create and enforce rules against free-riding and assure the long-term sustainability of communal properties. Her 'design principles' explain under what conditions this happens and when it fails. Furthermore, she also noted that cultural factors such as trust influence the amount of free-riding that one could expect to see. The importance of self-governance partially stems from this. The bottom line is that, while the rivalry aspect of a good is to a large extent objective, depending on the nature of the good itself, the social impact of the excludability aspect depends on the institutional system of formal rules and social norms. Consequently, the economic analysis of public goods and common-pool resources can be undertaken properly only from an institutionalist perspective that takes accounts of these factors.

Another important theoretical extension of standard economic theory is the concept of co-production. It became obvious in these common-pool resource studies that the consumer was often part of the production process: the standard economic separation between the producer who sells a product and the consumer who buys it was not tenable. But once one understands this idea of a 'consumer-producer' (i.e. a consumer actively involved in the production process, but who also pays something to the 'regular producer', with whom he cooperates, for the product), one starts to see it everywhere: a video game does not entertain without it being played; a concert is not a success if the public is completely passive; a professor cannot teach an unwilling or completely apathetic student; a doctor often needs the patient's inputs in the process of diagnosis; police cannot catch criminals if citizens are unwilling to provide them with any clues; fire protection services depend on the citizens' efforts to prevent fires; the justice system cannot function if no one is willing to be a witness, etc. Following the standard consumer theory framework, Ostrom and her collaborators created the basic mathematical model of co-production (Parks et al., 1981). From this model it follows that, when the regular producer and the consumer-producer are interdependent, as in the cases mentioned above, a trade-off emerges between the efforts of the regular producer and of the consumer-producer. The resulting outcome, how much is produced and the relative involvement of the regular producer and the consumer-producer depend on the relative costs encountered by them: the production costs (wages, and so on) paid by the regular producer versus the opportunity cost to the consumer of getting involved in the production process.

As Aligica and Boettke note '[t]he role of co-production came in many respects as a revelation', as it became obvious that the analysis of many public services was deficient because it ignored this issue. '[O]nce it was clearly defined, co-production problems could be identified in many sub-domains of the service industries in both private and public sectors ... It was the standard assumption of the separation of production from consumption that blinded everybody from identifying the source of what was called the "service paradox"' (2009: 33). The 'service paradox' consists of a situation in which '[t]he better services are, as defined by professional criteria, the less satisfied the citizens are with those services' (Ostrom and Ostrom, 1999 [1977]). This paradox emerges when the evaluation of the production process focuses solely on the part provided by the regular producer, ignoring the part played by the consumer-producer. Consequently, in such cases, the co-production trade-off is drifting away from its optimum and the interaction between the two parts is becoming more and more defective, despite genuine efforts to improve the service. To give a simple example, education may become worse, despite genuine improvements in textbooks and in classroom materials, if those developments undermine student motivation in some way, perhaps by presenting material so clearly that students no longer feel the need to discuss issues with classmates and teachers.

Polycentricity

Finally, the concept of *polycentricity* can be understood as the coexistence of many decision centres with autonomous and sometimes overlapping prerogatives, some of them organised at differing scales, and operating under an overarching set of rules. Polycentricity differs from anarchy in that the interactions between the decision centres are governed by well-established rules.[5] Nonetheless, polycentricity differs from hierarchical organisation as well in that the different decision centres have specified areas of authority in regard to which they need not defer to others. As Elinor Ostrom explains more in her lecture, it is these areas of limited autonomy that create, at the local level, a structure of incentives favourable to building trust and also create a diverse environment favourable to discovering better solutions to problems. These solutions are less vulnerable to disturbances as the strengths of one part of the system can help overcome the weaknesses of another part. In polycentric systems, users of common-pool resources 'achieve many of the advantages of utilizing local knowledge as well as the redundancy and rapidity of a trial-and-error learning process … information about what has worked well in one setting can be transmitted to others who may try it in their settings … and when small systems fail, there are larger systems to call upon – and vice-versa' (Ostrom, 1999: 39).

Fisheries: an application of Ostrom's work

To illustrate these concepts, let us briefly discuss a problem that affects Britain as well as many other countries: that of fisheries management. As Elinor Ostrom mentions in her lecture, the actual study of fisheries around the world has led to some surprises. For example, contrary to most economists' expectations, communities

---

5   Ostrom (1999); Ostrom (2005: ch. 9); Aligica and Boettke (2009: 101–7); McGinnis and Ostrom (2011); Aligica and Tarko (2012).

often do not regulate the quantity of fish that people are allowed to harvest, which can be too difficult to monitor, but instead rely on other proxies, such as regulating the allowed fishing time (for example, banning fishing during spawning periods), regulating the fishing location or the fishing technology (for example, banning 'overly efficient' technologies in certain parts of a river). The history of some of the US fisheries studied by Ostrom is interesting because of examples of how the intervention of the state can be both beneficial and deleterious.[6]

The Maine lobster fisheries were severely depleted in the 1920s, as local communities were failing in their attempts to effectively manage the fisheries. The state intervened by threatening some of the fisheries with closure, but, rather than setting up its own top-down comprehensive fishery policy, it merely 'supported informal local enforcement efforts'. The intervention was successful and 'by the late 1930s, compliance problems were largely resolved and stocks had rebounded'.

A more recent state intervention was to transform the informal local organisations which were beginning to break down into formalised councils with democratic local elections and formalised authority over specified geographical areas. This had an unexpected beneficial consequence when 'the formalization of local zones was followed, almost immediately, by the creation of an informal council of councils to address problems at a greater than local scale'. This highlights something that is often surprising to many: that cooperation between communities with regard to large-scale problems can often emerge from bottom up.

Another interesting example is that of Washington State

---

6   The following two paragraphs are based on Ostrom (1999).

Pacific salmon fisheries. Prior to the mid-1970s, they were centrally managed and, as Ostrom notes, they faced a typical knowledge problem: the 'centrally regulated system had focused on aggregations of species and spent little time on the freshwater habitats that are essential to maintain the viability of salmon fisheries over the long term'. In the mid-1970s, the management system changed owing to a major court decision that granted to 'Indian tribes that had signed treaties more than a century before' the right 'to 50 per cent of the fish that passed through the normal fishing areas of the tribes'. Consequently, '[t]his has required the state to develop a "co-management" system that involves both the state of Washington and the 21 Indian tribes in diverse policy roles related to salmon'. The change created a new system of incentives at the local level. On the one hand, the state's continued involvement assured the individual tribes that free-riding by other tribes was not going to be tolerated and, therefore, that their conservation efforts were worthwhile. On the other hand, the co-management system gave individual tribes an important economic stake in the resource, which, in turn, stimulated them to solve the aforementioned knowledge problem.

Other authors who have studied many other cases of successful or unsuccessful fisheries have also concurred that 'a better outcome is more likely with the right incentives, increasingly restrictive access, simpler institutions and appropriate management scales' (Hilborn et al., 2005: 53), and that 'fisheries management problems are strongly linked to distributive bargaining conflicts between small-scale and large-scale interests', a major stumbling block coming from the 'perceptions that prospective reforms will favor one segment of the fishing industry over the other' (Alcock, 2002: 459).

Conclusion

Summing up, Elinor Ostrom's contributions, as part of the Bloomington school, have challenged in important ways the conventional expert wisdom about the ways in which communities work and social cooperation emerges or fails. These contributions have led to a very important theoretical development – the construction of the IAD framework, and the associated theory of society as an interacting system of action arenas. As mentioned earlier, this theoretical development is in many ways an extension and generalisation of previous theories, especially public choice theory. As the Ostroms mention (Ostrom and Ostrom, 2004), this entire theoretical enterprise has its analytical roots in Buchanan and Tullock's *Calculus of Consent*, but it has since expanded considerably into a full-blown economic theory of society as a whole.

References

Alcock, F. (2002), 'Bargaining, uncertainty, and property rights in fisheries', *World Politics*, 54(4): 437–61.

Aligica, P. D. and P. J. Boettke (2009), *Challenging Institutional Analysis and Development: The Bloomington School*, New York: Routledge.

Aligica, P. D. and V. Tarko (2012), 'Polycentricity: from Polanyi to Ostrom, and beyond', *Governance*, 25(2): 237–62.

Boettke, P. J. (2001 [1996]), 'Why culture matters: economics, politics, and the imprint of history', in *Calculation and Coordination*, New York: Routledge, pp. 248–65.

Boettke, P. J., C. J. Coyne and P. T. Leeson (2008), 'Institutional stickiness and the new development economics', *American Journal of Economics and Sociology*, 67(2): 331–58.

Buchanan, J. M. and G. Brennan (2000 [1985]), *The Reason of Rules: Constitutional Political Economy*, Indianapolis: Liberty Fund.

Buchanan, J. M. and G. Tullock (1999 [1962]), *The Calculus of Consent*, Indianapolis: Liberty Fund.

Buchanan, J. M., R. D. Tollison and G. Tullock (eds) (1980), *Toward a Theory of the Rent-seeking Society*, Texas: A&M University Press.

Caplan, B. (2008), *The Myth of the Rational Voter: Why Democracies Choose Bad Policies*, new edn, Princeton, NJ: Princeton University Press.

Friedman, D. (2000), *Law's Order: What Economics Has to Do with the Law and Why It Matters*, Princeton, NJ: Princeton University Press.

Gaus, G. (2011), *The Order of Public Reason: A Theory of Freedom and Morality in a Diverse and Bounded World*, Cambridge: Cambridge University Press.

Giugni, M., D. McAdam and C. Tilly (eds) (1999), *How Social Movements Matter*, Minneapolis: University of Minnesota Press.

Goodwin, R. E. and C. Tilly (eds) (2006), *The Oxford Handbook of Contextual Political Analysis*, Oxford: Oxford University Press.

Hardin, G. (1968), 'The tragedy of the commons', *Science*, 162: 1243–8.

Harrison, J. L. (1995), *Law and Economics*, Eagan, MN: West Publishing Co.

Henrich, J. and F. Gil-White (2001), 'The evolution of prestige: freely conferred status as a mechanism for enhancing the benefits of cultural transmission', *Evolution and Human Behavior*, 22: 1–32.

Herald-Times (2009), 'The story of non-economist Elinor Ostrom', 9 December.

Hilborn, R., J. M. Orensanz and A. M. Parma (2005), 'Institutions, incentives and the future of fisheries', *Philosophical Transactions: Biological Sciences*, 360(1453): 47–57.

McGinnis, M. D. and E. Ostrom (2011), 'Reflections on Vincent Ostrom, public administration, and polycentricity', *Public Administration Review*, 72(1): 15–25.

Mueller, D. C. (1979), *Public Choice*, Cambridge: Cambridge University Press.

Olson, M. (1965), *Logic of Collective Action: Public Goods and the Theory of Groups*, Boston, MA: Harvard University Press.

Ostrom, E. (1990), *Governing the Commons: The Evolution of Institutions for Collective Action*, Cambridge: Cambridge University Press.

Ostrom, E. (1999), 'Polycentricity, complexity, and the commons', *Good Society*, 9(2): 37–41.

Ostrom, E. (2000), 'Collective action and the evolution of social norms', *Journal of Economic Perspectives*, 14(3): 137–58.

Ostrom, E. (2005), *Understanding Institutional Diversity*, Princeton, NJ: Princeton University Press.

Ostrom, E. (2008), 'Developing a method for analyzing institutional change', in S. Batie and N. Mercuro (eds), *Alternative Institutional Structures: Evolution and Impact*, New York: Routledge.

Ostrom, E. and V. Ostrom (2004), 'The quest for meaning in public choice', *American Journal of Economics and Sociology*, 63(1): 105–47.

Ostrom, V. (1997), *The Meaning of Democracy and the Vulnerabilities of Democracies: A Response to Tocqueville's Challenge*, Ann Arbor, MI: University of Michigan Press.

Ostrom, V. and Ostrom E. (1999 [1977]), 'Public goods and public choices', in M. D. McGinnis (ed.), *Polycentricity and Local Public Economies: Readings from the Workshop in Political Theory and Policy Analysis*, Ann Arbor, MI: University of Michigan Press.

Parks, R. B., P. C. Baker, L. L. Kiser, R. J. Oakerson, E. Ostrom, V. Ostrom, S. L. Percy, M. B. Vandivort, G. P. Whitaker and R. K. Wilson (1981), 'Consumers as coproducers of public services: some economic and institutional considerations', *Policy Studies Journal*, 9: 1001–11.

Richerson, P. and R. Boyd (2005), *Not by Genes Alone: How Culture Transformed Human Evolution*, Chicago, IL: University of Chicago Press.

Sperber, D. (1996), *Explaining Culture*, Oxford: Blackwell.

Tilly, C. (2003), *Contention and Democracy in Europe 1650–2000*, Cambridge: Cambridge University Press.

Tomasello, M. (2009), *Why We Cooperate*, Cambridge, MA: MIT Press.

Tullock, G. (2005), *The Selected Works of Gordon Tullock*, vol. 5: *The Rent-Seeking Society*, Indianapolis: Liberty Fund.

Tullock, G., A. Seldon and G. L. Brady (2002), *Government Failure: A Primer in Public Choice*, Washington, DC: Cato Institute.

Zagorski, N. (2006), 'Profile of Elinor Ostrom', *Proceedings of the National Academy of Sciences of the United States of America*, 103(51): 19221–3.

3 THE FUTURE OF THE COMMONS: BEYOND MARKET FAILURE AND GOVERNMENT REGULATION[1]

Elinor Ostrom

Introduction

Earlier studies of the commons focused on small-to-medium-sized common-pool resources, such as irrigation systems, fisheries and forests, into which we and many others undertook a great deal of research. But many of the studies of particular common-pool resources were by people working in a particular discipline without comparison with other studies and without any theoretical foundation.

But as we looked at those studies in our own research and as we did some empirical work, we were able to get a good sense of how small- and medium-sized common-pool resources were managed by common-property institutions. Now it turns out, especially after 2009, that there is considerable interest in our research on small, medium, large and global environmental systems. And researchers, citizens and officials are asking for some kind of a general framework that puts people and societies together and explains the ways in which they are able to manage common-pool resources.

When we put people and ecologies together, we can think of the results as a 'social-ecological system' (SES). Academic

---

1 The Hayek Memorial Lecture hosted by the IEA on 29 March 2012.

teams do not tend to share resources across disciplines, so that as you are trying to study these things you have to learn about the terminology from other disciplines. For example, I am now working with a group of ecologists studying forest resources and I had to learn what DBH meant (it is diameter breast height) and how to measure the size of a tree. I also had to learn a variety of other technical things because we are measuring the condition of the forests in a scientifically very careful way besides looking at the social systems and how they are organised.

Without understanding both the social systems and the technical aspects of the management of a resource, we cannot conduct work that enables us to understand the conditions that help produce sustainable management. We need to have a common framework of language that will enable us to help develop sustainable systems and achieve the sustainability of diverse commons.

Challenges in achieving sustainability

So what are some of the challenges that we face in achieving sustainability? The first one that I will talk about shortly is overcoming what I call the 'panacea trap'. A second one is developing a multidisciplinary, multi-tier framework for analysing sustainable social-ecological systems that people across disciplines can use. We need to build better theories for explaining and predicting behaviour. We need to find ways of collecting data over time, but we have got to learn which variables we should be studying in a consistent way to have good studies over time. And we need to understand design principles and why they work.

This is a very big agenda. They all point us to the importance of institutional diversity. In this lecture I will only be able to provide an overview of these, but I will be very glad to pursue one or another of them in questions if people want to do so.

Challenge one, as I mentioned, is the panacea problem. A very large number of policymakers and policy articles talk about 'the best' way of doing something. For many purposes, if the market was not the best way people used to think that it meant that the government was the best way. We need to get away from thinking about very broad terms that do not give us the specific detail that is needed to really know what we are talking about.

We need to recognise that the governance systems that *actually have worked in practice* fit the diversity of ecological conditions that exist in a fishery, irrigation system or pasture, as well as the social systems. There is a huge diversity out there, and the range of governance systems that work reflects that diversity. We have found that government, private and community-based mechanisms all work in some settings. People want to make me argue that community systems of governance are always the best: I will not walk into that trap.

There are certainly very important situations where people can self-organise to manage environmental resources, but we cannot simply say that the community is, or is not, the best; that the government is, or is not, the best; or that the market is, or is not, the best. It all depends on the nature of the problem that we are trying to solve.

Challenge two that we also need to be working on is the development of a multidisciplinary, multiple-tier framework for analysing social-ecological systems. And what we have done here is identify and analyse four very large encompassing variables that are at what we call a 'focal level'. These generate together an action situation in which individuals and groups interact and produce outcomes. When we talk about market relationships between buyers and sellers, we are looking at an action situation. And that focal level is affected by and affects larger and smaller ecosystems as well as larger and smaller social, economic and political systems.

So let us look at the first tier of that framework. We can think broadly of a resource system and a governance system – these are the sub-parts. A resource system sets conditions for an action situation, but we can think of resource units as part of that. So when we talk about a forest, part of the resource units are trees. If we talk about a fishery, the resource units are fish. They differ dramatically in their characteristics, but both are the resource unit that is being harvested.

We can also think of a wide diversity of actors who are participating in one or another of the action situations that affect the long-term sustainability of that system. They act within the governance system that sets the rules. This is a very broad framework, I am going to unpack it in a few minutes, but it is now being used by a number of people for current studies. So how does the framework help us build and test better theories?

That is the third challenge that we are facing. And the important thing is that the framework helps identify multiple variables that potentially affect the structure of action situations; the resulting interactions between the governance systems; the actions of the resource users and the resource system; and the outcomes in terms of the sustainable management of the resource.

And so this framework is one way that we can study similar systems that share some variables in common but that do not share all variables in common. It helps us to look at quite different systems. The framework then avoids the problem of people overgeneralising as they do in the literature, suggesting, for example, that all resources should be privately owned or that all resources should be government owned. If you read the original work on the tragedy of the commons, that was Garrett Hardin's conclusion. And in many contemporary textbooks, the Hardin argument is repeated.

There is also a problem of over-specification. Researchers can fall into the trap of pretending that their own cases are completely different from other cases. They refuse to accept that that there are lessons that one can learn from studying multiple cases. In reality, to diagnose why some social-ecological systems do self-organise in the first place and are robust, we need to study similar systems over time. We need to examine which variables are the same, which differ and which are the important variables so that we can understand why some systems of natural resource management are robust and succeed and others fail.

The importance of second-tier variables

Thus, part of our need is to look beyond the first tier of variables and to begin to develop the language more thoroughly by going on to examine a second tier of variables. Many of the second tiers have third and fourth tiers – but I am not going to get down to that level tonight: we are working on that diagnostic framework further. You can see a version of this in my 2009 *Science* article, and Mike McGinnis and I are currently working on a paper that is looking at all this.

Figure 2 shows the second-tier variables that are important under each first-tier variable for a social-ecological system. I am going to warn you that when people see this for the very first time,

Figure 2 Second-tier variables of an SES

Social, Economic, and Political Settings (S)
S1 – Economic development. S2 – Demographic trends. S3 – Political stability.
S4 – Government resource policies. S5 – Market incentives. S6 – Media organisation.

Resource Systems (RS)
RS1 – Sector (e.g., water, forests, pasture, fish)
RS2 – Clarity of system boundaries
RS3 – Size of resource system
RS4 – Human-constructed facilities
RS5 – Productivity of system
RS6 – Equilibrium properties
RS7 – Predictability of system dynamics
RS8 – Storage characteristics
RS9 – Location

Governance Systems (GS)
GS1 – Government organisations
GS2 – Nongovernment organisations
GS3 – Network structure
GS4 – Property-rights systems
GS5 – Operational rules
GS6 – Collective-choice rules
GS7 – Constitutional rules
GS8 – Monitoring and sanctioning rules

Resource Units (RU)
RU1 – Resource unit mobility
RU2 – Growth or replacement rate
RU3 – Interaction among resource units
RU4 – Economic value
RU5 – Number of units
RU6 – Distinctive characteristics
RU7 – Spatial and temporal distribution

Actors (A)
A1 – Number of actors
A2 – Socioeconomic attributes of actors
A3 – History of use
A4 – Location
A5 – Leadership/entrepreneurship
A6 – Norms (trust-reciprocity)/social capital
A7 – Knowledge of SES/mental models
A8 – Importance of resource (dependence)
A9 – Technology used

Action Situations: Interactions (I)
I1 – Harvesting
I2 – Information sharing
I3 – Deliberation processes
I4 – Conflicts
I5 – Investment activities
I6 – Lobbying activities
I7 – Self-organising activities
I8 – Networking activities
I9 – Monitoring activities
I10 – Evaluative activities

Outcomes (O)
O1 – Social performance measures
(e.g., efficiency, equity, accountability, sustainability)
O2 – Ecological performance measures
(e.g., overharvested, resilience, biodiversity, sustainability)
O3 – Externalities to other SESs

Related Ecosystems (ECO)
ECO1 – Climate patterns. ECO2 – Pollution patterns. ECO3 – Flows into and out of focal SES.

there is a kind of worried reaction at its complexity. This looks very complex. When you start thinking about what is involved in a resource system, you need to know what sector you are talking about (for example, forest, pasture, fish). You need to know where the clear boundaries for the resource are (for example, how are the boundaries defined if the resource is mobile?). You need to know how big the resource is, what kind of human-constructed facilities there are, and so on. Similarly, if you are going to talk about a governance system, we need to know whether we are talking about government organisations and about the kind of non-governmental organisations that could be involved in the governance system. We also need to think about the various kinds of property rights systems, the monitoring and sanctioning rules, and so on – all these things are very important. Then there are very important problems relating to the attributes of the resource units. For example, there is a difference between fish that move independently and fish that move in channels, and a difference between both of these types of resources and, for example, trees, which do not move at all.

And then there are the attributes of the kinds of actors involved. How many are there? What kind of socio-economic attributes do they have? What is their history of use of the resource? Where are the actors – are they in a similar location to the location of the resource, or in places far away? What kind of leadership is there? And so on.

This framework for the management of the commons is a broad framework, just like when you learn economic theory more generally. You do not need to look at all the variables in an economic theory for all the questions that you are going to look at. You need to learn how to pick out the variables that are important for the analysis of particular questions.

This approach does give us a sense of some of the variables that have been identified repeatedly as being important when determining whether people are able to govern a resource and do so sustainably. They are useful for that purpose.

Questions that can be addressed in our research framework

We can address three broad sets of questions within this research framework. The first set examines the patterns of interactions and outcomes that you might expect from a given set of rules for the governance and use of a particular resource system. This includes the question of how much overuse there will be; what kind of conflict there is likely to be among those governing the system; and whether a system with a particular set of attributes is likely to collapse or not. In other words, we are looking to find which rules generate sustainable outcomes for particular kinds of resources and looking at how to distinguish different kinds of resources that require different rules for their management. What we have learned is that the rules that are often used with regard to grasslands and pastoral institutions often generate overuse and collapse. We need to understand which ones do that and why. We need to understand which rules generate adaptation. And we need a framework of that sort to develop good research and good theories as we move along.

The second type of question is for a particular resource in a particular setting. What is the likely endogenous development of different governance arrangements, use patterns and outcomes with and without externally imposed rules or financing? This helps us to answer the important question of whether we need to impose institutions from outside.

We have been studying irrigation systems and forestry resources around the world. I have just finished a paper with an Indian colleague looking at the lakes in Bangalore in an urban area and comparing their sustainability. We need to know when we can expect the local people to be able to develop their own rules so that we know when to worry about whether a particular situation is one in which we are going to need to impose rules from outside. In what situations are the local people going to develop well-tailored rules of their own and how do we predict that they are going to do so? This depends on the autonomy of people living in a particular setting and using a resource, and their history.

The third type of question is how robust and sustainable is a particular configuration of users, resource systems, resource units and governance systems to external and internal disturbances? In other words, we need to look at the long-term sustainability both of resource units and governance, what kind of disturbances – such as climate change or population change – we are potentially going to see and whether we need to worry about them.

So all three of these are part of a long-term and big research programme, but all of them are enhanced by having a common framework for understanding social-ecological systems and the management of natural resources.

In researching these problems, a major challenge is to find comparable data over time for testing theories. This is another situation where challenges in terms of doing research are exacerbated by very tall walls between disciplines in terms of approaches and language. People do studies coming from one academic discipline and those studies can be very hard for someone in a different discipline to understand. As such, we need a common taxonomy of core variables in the social-ecological framework that will help us build more empirical research that we can all study.

Individual researchers have written a large number of individual case studies, but there has not been as much accumulation of scientific knowledge as we need. We need a large number of case studies because we see such variation between situations where natural resources are managed. If the variation is across only one or two variables, you do not need a large number of studies. But when you find more than a hundred different combinations of variables, as we have, you need large, large studies.

One of the initial things that we have been doing over time has been to study these cases and these combinations of variables. We developed a database early on in which we coded a lot of information about irrigation systems and fisheries. I thought that I was going to be able to analyse a series of cases using statistical analysis, but found out that I had to move up in my level of generality and look at a broader way of thinking about the problem. Instead of the details of a boundary rule, we had to look at whether they had a boundary rule at all. Instead of the details of collective-choice mechanisms that they might use, we had to ask whether they had the right to make their own rules and so on.

Design principles for the management of natural resource systems

Back in the 1980s, my co-researchers and I were struggling to try to find statistical relationships between features of social-ecological systems and outcomes. I developed a series of rules that were more general than specific, having failed to find the specific rules that were always successful in terms of producing sustainable outcomes for the management of a natural resource. I called these general rules 'design principles'. At times, I think that I should have called them something else because people confused that term with the idea that we are trying to design something from the beginning. However, I was really undertaking a study of robustness of systems that already existed. I presented the principles, which are discussed in great detail, in my 1990 book *Governing the Commons*.

I am very pleased to report that Cox, Arnold and Tomas have finished a very interesting article, published in *Ecology and Society* in 2010, where they searched the literature for people who had overtly studied whether or not the design principles that we identified actually characterised the case studies that they were looking at.

People had indeed done studies, and the authors looked at whether or not the management of a resource was successful and whether the design principles were helpful in bringing about that success. Cox, Arnold and Tomas looked at more than ninety studies and they did find very strong empirical support for the original design principles. The authors then suggested a better way of framing the design principles than I had done originally. For example, when I talked about boundary rules, I did not make a distinction between a clear set of boundaries of the resource and a clear set of boundaries for the users. Sometimes systems have clear boundaries for the resources but not for the users or vice versa and, in some of the case studies that were reported, that was a problem. So Cox, Arnold and Tomas crafted and clarified three of the design principles. They distinguished between clear boundaries of the resource users (that is the membership) and clear boundaries of the resource itself. So hopefully we will use that in our future work.

A second design principle is congruence with local and environmental conditions. Here, I am talking about the distribution of benefits and costs to the social structure, and I did not distinguish between the social part and the ecological part as Cox, Arnold and Tomas have.

In terms of monitoring, they distinguished monitoring of the resource conditions as well as monitoring of users' actions. Besides the boundaries and congruence and monitoring, my original design conditions also talked about graduated sanctions, conflict-resolution mechanisms and a recognition of the right of users to make their own rules, and, if it was a larger system, whether it was nested. They found very strong support for all of these and no need to distinguish them over time.

One important question is, why do the design principles work? Why do they enhance institutional robustness? One thing that we find is that the participants in a system that is characterised by the design principles know that the rules are being followed by others because they are monitored. A second reason is that those who are most knowledgeable about the effects of what is going to happen are the ones who are making the rules. A third is that they lead to a system where it is possible to resolve conflicts before they escalate.

We also find that a diversity of governance units trying to solve a fishery or irrigation or other resource problem stimulates learning and increases performance over time. And, as you study these things over time, you see people passing information about how they are doing and about why what they are doing is working. We find that both large and small units back each other up. So that is one of the important sets of findings from our research.

What have we learned?

In general, then, what have we learned? The attributes of the users that are conducive to their self-organising and managing a resource sustainably include that the users ask questions and that they view the resource as highly salient. They then usually have a relatively low discount rate in terms of the benefits obtained from the resource so that they are not over-exploiting the resource in the current time period. Over time, the users have developed high levels of trust and reciprocity and have the autonomy to determine at least some of their own rules. They are nested in complementary, multiple-tier systems. Usually in these kinds of settings, those organising the system have prior organisational experience; they have well-developed social capital and they have local leaders who are able to take on that very tough job. They also share some common understanding about the resource. These are the attributes that we are finding in systems that are sustainable.

At the same time, we are finding that the rules devised by self-organising communities differ in important ways from a lot of our traditional textbook remedies. For example, many of the textbook recommendations for regulating fisheries, if they are not for government to regulate them, are for individual transferable quotas. The key thing, it is argued, is regulating the quantity of the quota allocated. Yet, what we find in practice in many self-managed fisheries is that the fishers regulate the time when users of the resource can go and fish and they regulate the space where it is appropriate to harvest and the technology that should be used. The sustainable remedies in practice differ from the traditional textbook solutions, so those managing resources in practice are actually using different attributes from those suggested in the literature. Many of the rules that people develop or their methods of interrelationship are designed to encourage growth of trust and reciprocity. They tend to rely on unique aspects of a local resource and the local culture when developing their approach to managing the resource.

The relationship between larger and smaller units of governance

We also find that larger regimes can facilitate local self-organisation so that we are not thinking about little tiny units self-organising without any relationship to larger units. And very large units can be important in providing accurate scientific information to help the smaller units interact. For example, in the groundwater basin that I studied in southern California, the national United States Geological Survey has done some important research that helps local people figure out the boundaries of their resource.

Larger jurisdictions can also provide important conflict resolution. For example, court systems provided by larger jurisdictions are very important for helping resolve basic conflicts. Larger jurisdictions can provide technical assistance, which is effective if they view the local users as partners. It is important that they do not just assume that the locals do not know very much and tell them what to do! If there is some respect for the local user, the technical information provided by larger units can be very helpful. And the larger units can provide mechanisms for backing up monitoring and sanctioning efforts.

We have also looked at larger units that are donor-assisted units that are supported through the US government via USAID and by development agencies of one kind or another. We conducted a major study of them and produced a book entitled *The Samaritan's Dilemma*. What we found is that, tragically, they do not have a good foundation based on either theoretical or empirical knowledge. They frequently encourage a national government to give resources back to local people. But the resources have been taken away, degraded and then given back in a one- or two-hour meeting. I have been to some of those meetings and it is rather incredible. They bring the local people into a hall. They say 'now you own x'; they give them a little bit of background of what they must do now; tell the people that they are responsible; and then walk away.

Frequently in these kinds of situations, the governments retain formal ownership so that they are not passing on the ownership but only the management. Furthermore, they expect the users to perform rapidly what government agencies have not been able to do for years. So there is a very grim history out there in terms of donor-assisted handover projects of natural resource systems to local people.

One of the things that we have repeatedly found is the importance of what we call polycentric systems. This is where systems exist at multiple levels, with some autonomy at each level. So, we can think about a region where there is a government agency responsible for the large region, but there is a lot of local autonomy in the management of local resources in that region. If we create a polycentric system, then it retains many of the benefits of local-level systems because there are people at a local level making decisions about many of the rules. But it also adds overlapping units to help monitor performance, obtain reliable information and cope with large-scale resources. Indeed, I argue very strongly for the need for polycentric institutions to cope with climate change.

Conclusion

I have given you a very rapid overview of a vast amount of research. The final question is, so what? One of the things that we have found in our large-scale studies, much to the surprise of many people, is that local monitoring is one of the most important factors affecting resource conditions and the success of resource management systems in fisheries, pastures, forestry, water and so on. We now have studies published in *Science* on our forestry work, looking at situations where nobody was thinking that local users could be important monitors. But we examine this because we have found it so important in many studies. The local people pay attention to what is happening in the forest if they have some rights to collect. Local users are in the forest from time to time, and monitoring is not very expensive when it is done in this way. If you have to hire government officials to be the monitors, that is very expensive. And frequently, when you hire government officials, they cannot be paid very much so you have problems of corruption.

We are now working with colleagues on the social-ecological systems framework. We continue to fine-tune the framework, and will have reports on about ten updated studies in a special issue that is forthcoming later this year or the beginning of next year in the journal *Ecology and Society*.

We are also working on getting definitions of key terms done, and how this affects the development of theories. We are studying forestry, water resources and fisheries over time. We are trying to study which propositions hold with regard to diverse resources on diverse scales. So, that has given you a very fast overview.

4 QUESTIONS AND DISCUSSION

MATTIA BACCIARDI: I heard words like 'flexibility', 'adaptability', 'trust', 'reciprocity', 'social capital', 'self-organisation' and they seem to be actually applied to the society as a whole rather than just to specific commons such as fisheries and pastures. Wouldn't it be possible to interpret your theory as being a theory of social organisation as a whole?

PROFESSOR OSTROM: Well, at one level the polycentricity aspect is certainly one that is capable of being widely applied. It isn't that there is a single set of rules that will work in all places in a particular society. So, if we talk about local fisheries that evolved in Turkey, those rules are quite specific to local inshore fisheries and to Turkish fishermen and they are quite different from those that would work in the USA and a variety of other places. So yes, what we are trying to think through is ways that people facing problems on diverse scales can self-organise and cope more effectively with managing those resources over the long run.

ANIOL ESTEBAN: I am very interested in fish. At the New Economics Foundation we are working a lot on fish. It is a very interesting year for fish, particularly in Europe where the Common Fisheries Policy is being reviewed. The question is, looking at the state of European fish stocks today which are pretty bad ...

PROFESSOR OSTROM: Terrible.

ANIOL ESTEBAN: Terrible. Based on all your experience with the fisheries system, would you have two or three general rules about how we can sort out EU Fisheries?

PROFESSOR OSTROM: Well, it is rather tragic because the European fisheries rules go all the way from the Mediterranean to the Baltic. And it's one set of rules for all that. The Baltic is an entirely different ecological system and it just doesn't make sense.

There will be an article to be published very soon – I've seen a version in print. The author headed a research team studying a large number of community-managed fisheries that had different kinds of rules, and so on. And they were able to look at community-managed, government-managed and open access. Open access was terrible. They looked at things like the income that the fishermen were receiving, how long their seasons were, a variety of things. And they used very careful measures of the amount of fish in the water – they went diving and did measurement, very careful measurement. And they found that those fisheries that were community controlled were much more successful on a variety of fronts. And you might find that quite relevant.

The EU could be providing some very broad overarching ways of conflict resolution, but allowing people to self-organise in ways that they had done before we outlawed it. We have some similar problems in some parts of the USA. So it is not just the EU: this is a very big problem. But it needs a polycentric approach.

CHAIRMAN: Yes. I'm not sure that sounds like the EU but anyway good luck.

HUBERT SCHMITZ: I am from the Institute of Development Studies at Sussex. I have two questions. My first one is to what extent is the framework you set out suitable to come to grips with climate-change issues? My second question is does your work, the work of you and your colleagues, give us any handle on the time dimension? The unprecedented feature of the climate-change debate is that we are expected to find a solution by certain dates. This is not the case for many of the other collective action problems that we have. Do you give us an analytical handle on this time dimension in any way?

PROFESSOR OSTROM: In the framework we are talking about, there are a number of characteristics about the resource system that do affect the time dimension. We have applied the framework to lakes, pasture areas, fisheries and a variety of modest resources. It has not yet been applied to climate change but it can be. And my sense is that we have modelled climate change inappropriately. We have modelled it as if the only externality of actions is global. And so when you take actions that produce greenhouse gases, you are producing a single externality and it goes all the way up.

Well, many of the externalities affect a family, a local neighbourhood, a region, a city, or other units. As more and more of the local units have begun to recognise that, they have taken various actions to encourage locals to reduce greenhouse gases. Now that's not sufficient but it can be as we get more and more locals doing it. We now have over a thousand mayors in the USA that have signed an agreement to start working on various ways of reducing greenhouse gases in their cities.

A thousand cities is quite different from just one. And we have a number of things that are going on that we do need to do at the global level. I am not arguing against that, but I am very nervous about just sitting around and waiting and making the argument that the rest of us can't do anything at all. So we need global action, but we can be taking action at multiple scales. And the cumulative effect of that does reduce greenhouse gas emissions.

SPEAKER: I have a general methodological question about theories of learning governance which appear in social sciences generally. There is a problem with learning and transmission of communication and information in those theories. For example, many countries spend millions of pounds or dollars on environmental impact assessments, looking at the cross-border detrimental impact on the environment of cross-border trade. But there is no incentive for each system (for example, between Canada and America) to learn from the other system about what is effective and what is not.

You talked about diversity and learning. What is it methodologically that you've factored in which allows these disparate systems to learn from each other? How do you get an incentive, for example with environmental impact assessments, for each of these countries to learn from each other rather than wasting millions of pounds of taxpayers' money down the tube when all the systems are ineffective.

PROFESSOR OSTROM: One of the ways is trying to enhance associations of resource governance. So in Nepal, we now have a farmer-managed Irrigation System Association and they are meeting regularly. Each year there's an award for innovation and new practices. And there is sharing of both successes and failures. So the question is, how do people learn? A lot of the learning in more traditional society occurred in the marketplace. So people would observe fish coming into the market that were in great shape and they would ask each other 'What are you doing?' And we can think about the slow evolution of rule systems where people learn from one that works and can try it out without changing everything in their own system. So it is a question of how we create environments where it's very easy for information exchange about conditions, size, rules, etc.

CHRIS BAIN: I work for a British development NGO. Thank you very much for your framework which I thought was really helpful. Would you agree that minerals are part of the commons? And, if so, could the framework help avoid what Professor Paul Collier calls the plunder of many minerals by arrangements between corrupt governments in the South and some mining companies? And, thirdly, would you agree that transparency in the way that business and governments work is a prerequisite for your framework working?

PROFESSOR OSTROM: Let me turn to the last question. Transparency is very important. Being able to get a good idea of what is the boundary, who is involved, what rules are involved is essential. And successful systems use a variety of mechanisms to keep the cost of sharing that information as low as possible. If you have a twenty-page rule document, that's not very transparent. But many of the successful systems don't have huge rule systems but everyone around knows quite carefully what they must or must not do.

In terms of minerals I haven't thought very much about it. Minerals in the ground come very close to private goods. But I would have to do some deep thinking about it. Oil in the ground has the problem of being a commons even though we have not treated it as such very much. Most of the resources that I have looked at are generally renewable. And one of the very difficult problems about minerals is that they are non-renewable. But I have not really studied them. It's a good question.

DAVID DUNN: I am very interested in natural resource taxes and I have been proposing those for a long time but there seems to be very little information on it. And what you are saying about the commons is very similar to what I am saying but stretching right across, into minerals and all the natural resources.

My question really is this. Do we not have to wake up and really think about taxing the pollution that all the resources are actually producing? My suggestion is that we need to think about taxing the resources in a way that reflects scientists' views of the environmental damages caused by the various resources and then tax them at source. This would replace the taxes that we are paying at the moment: so my proposal is substitution, we would not be paying more taxes. So I am just wondering if you are thinking anything along those lines as well.

PROFESSOR OSTROM: If the tax goes to a national government and is lost in the big volume of tax income and is not in any way retained to try to affect the source of the pollution, taxing may make a tiny difference but not a very significant one. It is how we allow resources to go back. So, if a river system, or any of the resources we might look at, is organised and the taxes are imposed by a bigger unit but a very substantial proportion goes back to the unit that is managing the resource for the purpose of reducing the harm then taxes can make a difference.

NICK COWEN: Listening to your talk, it struck me that your idea to solve some of these problems at a research level requires you to have these multilayered, multidisciplined, multidisciplinary research projects and teams. I was wondering if, in some ways, this was actually quite similar to some of the things that you are studying in that you're dealing with people who have a number of different motivations, drawing on common resources and have different ends in themselves. But, at the same time, they are trying to reach a common goal. And so I was wondering if you had found that your analysis was actually useful for studying some of your own work and potentially how universities and other academic projects and academic teams operate. This would certainly be very interesting in my line of work.

PROFESSOR OSTROM: We do interdisciplinary work. We have frequently had quite a struggle in our own universities and people have asked why Vincent [Ostrom] and I formed something called a workshop: the Workshop in Political Theory and Policy Analysis. It has been interdisciplinary from the beginning, but the idea was that if you were really going to do good science you needed seniors, juniors and young people working together.

We had been making furniture with a cabinetmaker in a workshop. And I watched the whole process of young people learning the skill – and in some cases a junior person showing a more senior person a better idea so that it wasn't all top down. One of Vincent's articles in the late 1970s was on science as artisanship discussing how we need to find ways of working as teams. And so that is partly related to what you are talking about.

If you are going to be doing the kind of research that some of us are doing where the fieldwork is very exhausting and very challenging, and you are producing only part of a database, you have got to have trust; you are building something that is productive for all of you. There is a similarity with managing a commons.

DEREK WALL: You have made a huge contribution getting us thinking about property which isn't private or state; and people can't quite cope with that. And you have also flagged up the idea of usufruct: that you have property rights as long as you maintain them.

I want to ask you two questions around this. You look at discrete commons with boundaries or have in the past. I am interested in 'inter-commoning'. So I think of North America where you've got indigenous groups with overlapping territories, you know of similar things in India. So has there been research on inter-commoning and on how different commons regimes can overlap? Also, a lot of your work is based on history. What questions should environmental historians be asking to take forward research into common pool property?

PROFESSOR OSTROM: Using the framework would be one way. Some of the history has been about a region – say Africa. But things that historians have found about Asia are not known by historians studying Africa. And so there are missing variables going across. So that is one problem.

And the ... the very first part of your question ... Intellectually it is a shared commons that we are struggling to understand and part of the reason for trying to develop a common language is that, if all of our descriptions use different languages, then we are not sure of what they mean. And so we are trying slowly but surely to get a common language. Part of the need for all of those variables is that, if you are going to be talking about fishery systems, there are certain of the attributes that are very, very important. With regard to the resource units there may be differences but, with regard to the governance and actors it may be very similar to a water system.

There will be about eight studies in that *Ecology and Society* special issue examining diverse kinds of resources using the framework. And we're not settled yet. We meet about once or twice a year and we have been addressing subtle changes so that we can make it better and better over time.

SPEAKER: I am from a local government think tank. I thought it was interesting that on one of your slides you asked whether we need to worry about imposing institutions from the outside. So I was wondering how you see the dynamic interaction between exogenous monitoring and imposition of institutions with the development of local governance structures and local monitoring.

PROFESSOR OSTROM: This is again a polycentric need. We should find ways of getting information for a large number of small systems that are aggregated. And we should look at it not always in terms of the aggregated outcomes. This may not be something that you can ask locals to do.

Colin Clark's recent work on fishery systems looked at what

happened when people got firm rights – sometimes the individual transferable quota to a particular species. So you have a right to harvest shrimp or tuna or whatever. And people were throwing the by-catch over the side of the ship. So they would catch a bunch of fish, sort through, keep what was the valuable fish for which they had a quota, and throw everything else away. That is very destructive, but many, many systems that have tried individual transferable quotas had that kind of problem.

In British Colombia they developed a new system so that if you receive a quota you must have a government observer on your boat. You have to pay the cost of that observer. It is very expensive but that person then records everything whenever you take fish out of the west coast ocean. And the temptation to take by-catches and then throw them away is gone because it's illegal and there is an observer.

So sharing information and very close monitoring – you wouldn't always want to monitor that closely – is important. In this case, the profit from the abuse of the rules was very large and the over-harvesting was immense and so to protect the fishery you had to do something like this.

LINDA WHETSTONE: At the end under your 'So what?' heading you wrote and you said: 'The most effective rule enforcements I have undertaken in community-governed resources are by the users themselves.' You added 'if they have rights', which I imagine is rather crucial. Could you give us one or two examples?

PROFESSOR OSTROM: Again, going back to fishery systems, there are local inshore fisheries that have evolved their own systems but they don't have firm rights. National governments can come along and say 'nothing but government-authorised fisheries and fishers are allowed in our community' and things that have taken a hundred years or so to evolve are just eliminated. That's happened in fisheries and it's happened in forestry a lot.

In India, indigenous peoples evolved rules for managing forest resources over the centuries. Then, when India was first conquered, the bureaucrats developed and imposed rules, many of which were learned from German sources (because a great deal of the early effort of managing forestry was done in Germany). The Indian government bought into a good deal of that set of rules and so it kicked people out of areas where they had managed forests for long periods of time. They declared them government-owned and then, since they were government-owned, the government could decide which parties could use the resource. And sometimes that meant that it was used privately and a number of companies came in and harvested like mad and wrecked earlier systems that had evolved over very long times.

SHANE MAHEN: Resource wealth can be both a blessing and a curse. Unfortunately, across much of Africa, it hasn't delivered the prosperity that it is very much capable of. I wanted to know about your opinion on the framework, politically and economically, which has been holding back the creation of wealth which resources can deliver in Africa. In the near future can these extractive industries be managed to allow a sustainable approach?

PROFESSOR OSTROM: It is very hard after people have been told that they are stupid and that they don't understand and you've taken their rights away. You can't just, all of a sudden, hand it back and expect that to produce automatic results. As I indicated, in some of the government programmes that are trying to hand resources back they do so in a general meeting, and that's about it.

That doesn't mean that it isn't possible in parts of Africa to really help people evolve better institutions. We have wonderful colleagues at Makerere University in Uganda who are doing some excellent studies. And we found in the Kampala area some very clever evolved institutions that had worked for long periods of time. Then, all of a sudden, people were very excited about 'decentralisation'. Many of the government districts were supposedly decentralised, but what that meant was unclear to the officials and to the people who had been managing the resource. The resource had not really been managed by a larger government, but their presumption was that it had been; and now it was being decentralised to a local area. What they have found is that this process actually took powers away from locals because these new officials hired at a local level did not know about evolved systems out there in the countryside. And it created chaos.

And as we talked earlier about the importance of knowledge and trust, if you don't know who is involved and who is going to be the official that you have to go to when there's a conflict etc. then that reduces your capacity to organise. But there are many, many settings in Africa where people have self-organised and are doing very well. But it's rough when governments are adopting policies that make it difficult to do so.

HILARY WAINWRIGHT: Could applied human creativity be considered a commons? In a sense, it seems an appropriate area for going beyond the market and going beyond being treated as a commodity, but also for going beyond regulation and government command. Could your particularly grounded methodology provide a way of thinking about the governance of applied human creativity – labour – to avoid wastage, exhaustion, to encourage nourishment and development? Obviously it can't be treated in the abstract and it's different in the sense that it's individual and social and it is self-reflexive in a way. But I just wondered whether work has been part of your thinking.

PROFESSOR OSTROM: No. But we can be thinking about the teams of people who do solve these problems, having to figure out how to pay each other and things of this sort. Many of the rules have to do with who gets resources when, where and how and whether they have to have shown certain kinds of inputs prior to that. But we have not actually looked at labour as a commons.

5 OSTROM'S IDEAS IN ACTION

Christina Chang

Andean peasant farmers are obviously unlikely to be familiar with Elinor Ostrom's ideas on governance of the commons. Yet their system for managing the local environment to promote their livelihoods provides an informative case study of her principles for governing common-pool resources. Applying Ostrom's ideas also gives insights to guide interventions by non-governmental organisations (NGOs), such as CAFOD,[1] and more importantly to guide governments and international institutions which often design the framework in which these communities operate.

The congruence between Ostrom's ideas and the way in which Andean farmers practise should not be surprising as Elinor Ostrom made several research visits to the area during her career. The success of the farmers in working in harmony with a difficult climate and thereby ensuring their own food security could not have escaped her. The importance of the socio-political organisation in the success of the farmers' approach would also not have surprised Elinor Ostrom (Regalsky and Hosse, 2008). These community-based approaches to the management of natural resources in the highland communities of the Andean region in which CAFOD works are increasingly under threat from often well-intentioned reforms and innovations, including those promoted by NGOs.

---

1   CAFOD is a Catholic charity and aid agency that focuses on providing help to the poorest peoples of the world.

The Andean communities with which CAFOD works have their own normative framework to ensure the right conditions for their productive strategies. This includes establishing norms for access to communal resources – notably water, land and biogenetic materials (seeds and crop materials) – and norms for regulating coexistence, ownership and the sharing of labour among families (ibid.). Their system dates back over two thousand years to pre-Hispanic times (Murra, 1975) and has survived the introduction of plantations and industrial agriculture, partly because of the isolation of these populations who live at an altitude higher than three thousand metres. In this situation there is a clearly defined communal resource as required by Ostrom's first design principle.

A further design principle – that rules governing the use of resources should be adapted to local conditions – is not only satisfied, but is central to the communities' success. The rules can even be interpreted as a codification of centuries of knowledge of managing their unique local resources and adapting to difficult climatic conditions in their local environment (Albó, 1989; Delgado, 2002).

Land is communally owned and its use is communally decided by the *sindicato*, made up of the community members. A soil rotation system allows the community to make the most of land that is particularly varied in quality. The starting point is a traditional system of soil classification based on subsoil type, how rocky the land is, the depth of cover, gradient and altitude. Communal lands are divided into sections called *mantas*, *aynuqas* (from which the management system often takes its name), *aytas* and *lames* (Harris, 1987). Each year the assembly decides which sections to cultivate through a rotation cycle which lasts around three years and consists of planting potatoes, followed by grains and finally leaving the land fallow. The rotation order and which fallow lands are used for grazing are determined communally according to needs, conditions and availability of appropriate soil types. This system allows communities to maximise yields under prevailing conditions, minimise risks by adapting use to several different microclimates and prevent damage either to crops by grazing or to soil by inappropriate use (Hervé, 1994).

Communal management of the land also allows the community to make best use of their labour resources (CENDA, 2008). The communities have a rule of *ayni* or *umraqa:* that is reciprocity. Owing to irregular rainfall, combined with a lack of irrigation systems, farmers may need to call on a larger workforce at unpredictable times. Under the system of *umraqa* a farmer can call on relatives and neighbours with whom he has ties to work during this period, and will later pay them back in an equivalent way. This overcomes the problem of sporadically needing more intensive labour in a system based on household working (Calvo et al., 1994).

The ability to undertake collective decision-making – another of Ostrom's design principles – is not just a management tool, it is essential to food security and survival. A good illustration of the link between the practical and the political is the use of weather predictions by the community in their planning. Farmers use animal and plant behaviour, astrological signs and the practice of rites to forecast whether there will be frost, hail, drought or floods. However, no single farmer's prediction is taken as correct; collective decisions are based on combined predictions of the group of farmers. This proves to be an effective tool in improving accuracy and managing risk (Morlon et al., 1982). Peruvian peasant farmers were found to be better than meteorological organisations at forecasting the effects of El Niño (IECTA, 2007), and farmers have been found to have successfully and accurately predicted when rains will arrive several months in advance (CENDA, 2007, 2008).

The next group of Ostrom's design principles deals with enforcement of the governance system: monitoring, conflict resolution and sanctions for those violating rules. Here again, the Andean farmers' systems conform to Ostrom's framework. The discipline and the control that the community can place on the land and its use is a fundamental element of the community's good functioning. The *sindicato* in high-altitude areas has the power, not only to grant lands, but also to take them away if they are not being used appropriately. For example, a farmer can lose his land if he fails to use it well or omits to fulfil his communal obligations. This can happen despite state-allocated ownership titles (Regalsky and Hosse, 2008).

Ostrom's final design principles relate to how the community's own organisation fits within a broader reality. She holds that the community's attempts at self-determination need to be recognised by higher authorities and that, where local resources are part of a larger resource, layers of organisations should build up from the small, local common-pool resource.

It is the breakdown of these design principles which lies at the heart of the crisis currently facing Andean farmers. While their traditions and community rules and practices are not outlawed by the Bolivian government, they are not supported either. Many interventions designed to improve their standard of living and their contribution to progress in one of Latin America's poorest countries are not undertaken in sympathy with their strategies and structures.

For example, agrarian land reform to put in place individual land titles, promoted notably by the World Bank, is threatening to disintegrate the community organisation that is the foundation of management of the productive system in this common territory with its heterogeneous nature (Schulte, 1996).

Other initiatives involve trying to promote more 'businesslike' organising principles in the practices of the Andean communities. There have been efforts to make farmers think more commercially – or competitively – and to seek to access markets on better conditions, get better prices than their neighbours, and so on. This has damaged community relations, generating disputes, damage by cattle and even *laycasqa* or spells being cast on neighbours (Regalsky and Hosse, 2008).

It would be a mistake to believe that this means that these communities are backward-looking or isolationist. This is simply not the case. For example, although some innovations, such as tractors, have not worked well in local conditions – reducing productivity of the *kupaya* potato crop in the Raqaypampa region by over 50 per cent over the course of twenty years (CENDA, 2005) – others have been adopted more happily. Irrigation methods work well with the soil-rotation system and allow the farmers to intensify production.

Also, a significant proportion of the production is destined for market. Though the study is now somewhat dated, as long ago as 1986/87 a study found that 27 per cent of produce was sent to market or exchanged for work or other goods or services (Regalsky and Hosse, 2008).

The productivity of peasant Andean agriculture is founded in its governance of common resources: rules that are rooted in centuries of knowledge of what works in local conditions and around which local communities are organised. To insist that increasing productivity relies solely on modernisation through chemical or industrial inputs, or commercial competition, not only threatens those livelihoods but also the environment and the very resources on which they depend. Modern technologies and market principles can enhance or undermine this productivity, depending on whether they respect the community system founded on governance of local resources or not.

Understanding this is central to CAFOD's programmes in Bolivia, where three out of five people in rural areas still live in extreme poverty and where impacts of climate change and efforts to exploit the country's significant natural resources are further undermining local livelihoods. CAFOD is supporting collaboration between University College London and local partners CIPCA and CENDA to better understand how this system works and to make the case for changes in strategies by the Bolivian government and others where these are needed.

Ostrom's design principles not only chime well with CAFOD's own Catholic principles of stewardship and the promotion of the common good, but also with the principle of subsidiarity whereby central government's main role is ensuring that the framework exists to help individuals, families and communities to pursue their legitimate objectives. It is not the role of government to displace community mechanisms of governance and organisation with its own structures. Ostrom's design principles also involve the distillation of the practical tools that are actually used to promote productivity and sustainability in a very unpromising environment.

References

Albó, X. (1989), *Para comprender las culturas rurales en Bolivia. Bolivia pluricultural y multilingüe*, La Paz: CIPCA, MEC, UNICEF.

Calvo, L. M., P. Regalsky, C. Espinoza and T. Hosse (1994), *Raqaypampa: Los complejos caminos de una comunidad andina*, Cochabamba: CENDA.

CENDA (2005), *Raqaypampa: Una experiencia de control territorial. Crisis agrícola y soberanía alimentaria*, Cochabamba: CENDA.

CENDA (2007), 'Waliq wata kananpaq señas willamun', *Conosur ñawpaqman*, 24: 12, http://www.cenda.org/periodico/126/126-sep-2007.pdf 11.12.08.

CENDA (2008), 'Papata iskay m'itapi churana kanqa', *Conosur ñawpaqman*, 25: 12, http://www.cenda.org/periodico/131/131-octubre-2008.pdf.

Delgado, J. M. F. (2002), *Estrategías de autodesarrollo y gestión sostenible del territorio en ecosistemas de montaña. Complementariedad ecosimbiótica en el Ayllu de Majsaya Mujlli*, 2nd edn, La Paz: Plural.

Harris, O. (1987), *Economía étnica*, La Paz: Hisbol.

Hervé, D. (1994), 'Desarrollo sostenible en los Andes altos. Los sistemas de cultivo con descanso largo pastoreado', in D. Hervé, D. Genin and G. Riviere (eds), *Dinámicas del Descanso de la Tierra en los Andes*, La Paz: IBTA-ORSTOM.

IECTA (2007), 'El Niño en la sierra central del Perú', *Revista electrónica Volveré*, http://www.unap.cl/iecta/revistas/volvere_26/articulo_2_volvere_26.htm 20.7.2008.

Morlon, P., B. Orlove and A. Hibon (1982), *Tecnologías agrícolas tradicionales en los Andes Centrales: perspectivas para el desarrollo*, Lima: UNESCO/UNDP/COFIDE.

Murra, J. (1975), 'El control vertical de un máximo de pisos ecológicos en la economía de las sociedades andinas', in J. Murra (ed.), *Formaciones Económicas y Políticas del Mundo Andino*, Lima: IEP.

Regalsky, P. and T. Hosse (2008), *Indigenous Peasant Strategies for Climate Risk Reduction in the Bolivian Andes*, London: CAFOD.

Schulte, M. (1996), *Tecnología Agrícola Altoandina, el manejo de la diversidad ecológica en el Valle de Charazani*, La Paz: Plural/ CID.

ABOUT THE IEA

The Institute is a research and educational charity (No. CC 235 351), limited by guarantee. Its mission is to improve understanding of the fundamental institutions of a free society by analysing and expounding the role of markets in solving economic and social problems.

The IEA achieves its mission by:

- a high-quality publishing programme
- conferences, seminars, lectures and other events
- outreach to school and college students
- brokering media introductions and appearances

The IEA, which was established in 1955 by the late Sir Antony Fisher, is an educational charity, not a political organisation. It is independent of any political party or group and does not carry on activities intended to affect support for any political party or candidate in any election or referendum, or at any other time. It is financed by sales of publications, conference fees and voluntary donations.

In addition to its main series of publications the IEA also publishes a termly journal, *Economic Affairs*.

The IEA is aided in its work by a distinguished international Academic Advisory Council and an eminent panel of Honorary Fellows. Together with other academics, they review prospective IEA publications, their comments being passed on anonymously to authors. All IEA papers are therefore subject to the same rigorous independent refereeing process as used by leading academic journals.

IEA publications enjoy widespread classroom use and course adoptions in schools and universities. They are also sold throughout the world and often translated/reprinted.

Since 1974 the IEA has helped to create a worldwide network of 100 similar institutions in over 70 countries. They are all independent but share the IEA's mission.

Views expressed in the IEA's publications are those of the authors, not those of the Institute (which has no corporate view), its Managing Trustees, Academic Advisory Council members or senior staff.

Members of the Institute's Academic Advisory Council, Honorary Fellows, Trustees and Staff are listed on the following page.

The Institute gratefully acknowledges financial support for its publications programme and other work from a generous benefaction by the late Alec and Beryl Warren.

107

Other papers recently published by the IEA include:

Taxation and Red Tape
The Cost to British Business of Complying with the UK Tax System
Francis Chittenden, Hilary Foster & Brian Sloan
Research Monograph 64; ISBN 978 0 255 36612 0; £12.50

Ludwig von Mises – A Primer
Eamonn Butler
Occasional Paper 143; ISBN 978 0 255 36629 8; £7.50

Does Britain Need a Financial Regulator?
Statutory Regulation, Private Regulation and Financial Markets
Terry Arthur & Philip Booth
Hobart Paper 169; ISBN 978 0 255 36593 2; £12.50

Hayek's *The Constitution of Liberty*
An Account of Its Argument
Eugene F. Miller
Occasional Paper 144; ISBN 978 0 255 36637 3; £12.50

Fair Trade Without the Froth
A Dispassionate Economic Analysis of 'Fair Trade'
Sushil Mohan
Hobart Paper 170; ISBN 978 0 255 36645 8; £10.00

A New Understanding of Poverty
Poverty Measurement and Policy Implications
Kristian Niemietz
Research Monograph 65; ISBN 978 0 255 36638 0; £12.50

The Challenge of Immigration
A Radical Solution
Gary S. Becker
Occasional Paper 145; ISBN 978 0 255 36613 7; £7.50

Sharper Axes, Lower Taxes
Big Steps to a Smaller State
Edited by Philip Booth
Hobart Paperback 38; ISBN 978 0 255 36648 9; £12.50

Self-employment, Small Firms and Enterprise
Peter Urwin
Research Monograph 66; ISBN 978 0 255 36610 6; £12.50

Crises of Governments
The Ongoing Global Financial Crisis and Recession
Robert Barro
Occasional Paper 146; ISBN 978 0 255 36657 1; £7.50

... and the Pursuit of Happiness
Wellbeing and the Role of Government
Edited by Philip Booth
Readings 64; ISBN 978 0 255 36656 4; £12.50

Public Choice – A Primer
Eamonn Butler
Occasional Paper 147; ISBN 978 0 255 36650 2; £10.00

The Profit Motive in Education: Continuing the Revolution
Edited by James B. Stanfield
Readings 65; ISBN 978 0 255 36646 5; £12.50

Which Road Ahead – Government or Market?
Oliver Knipping & Richard Wellings
Hobart Paper 171; ISBN 978 0 255 36619 9; £10.00

Other IEA publications

Comprehensive information on other publications and the wider work of the IEA can be found at www.iea.org.uk. To order any publication please see below.

Personal customers

Orders from personal customers should be directed to the IEA:
Clare Rusbridge
IEA
2 Lord North Street
FREEPOST LON10168
London SW1P 3YZ
Tel: 020 7799 8907. Fax: 020 7799 2137
Email: crusbridge@iea.org.uk

Trade customers

All orders from the book trade should be directed to the IEA's distributor:
Gazelle Book Services Ltd (IEA Orders)
FREEPOST RLYS-EAHU-YSCZ
White Cross Mills
Hightown
Lancaster LA1 4XS
Tel: 01524 68765. Fax: 01524 53232
Email: sales@gazellebooks.co.uk

IEA subscriptions

The IEA also offers a subscription service to its publications. For a single annual payment (currently £42.00 in the UK), subscribers receive every monograph the IEA publishes. For more information please contact:
Clare Rusbridge
Subscriptions
IEA
2 Lord North Street
FREEPOST LON10168
London SW1P 3YZ
Tel: 020 7799 8907. Fax: 020 7799 2137
Email: crusbridge@iea.org.uk